"Hardesty's book is especially valuable for church libraries because its short, lively sketches are easy for both youth and adults to enjoy. . . . Highly recommended."

—*Provident Book Finder*

"This book helps women to discover their 'roots' in the church and to realize that women throughout its history have confronted the same prejudices as do women today. . . . I strongly recommend this book to those women who are today struggling to discover their roles in the church."

—*The Church Herald*

"Hardesty . . . sets before the reader in concise biographical form the lives of more than twenty women, giving testimony to the balance in word and deed that has been the hallmark of Christian women down through the ages. . . . Thank you, Nancy, for shedding more light on a neglected subject!"

—*Evangelical Women's Caucus Update*

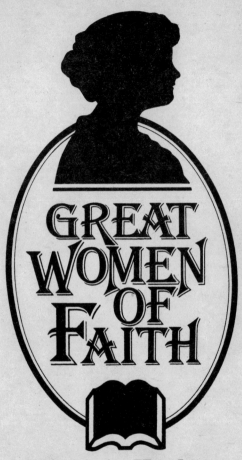

GREAT WOMEN OF FAITH

Nancy A. Hardesty

Abingdon  Nashville

GREAT WOMEN OF FAITH

A Festival Book

Copyright 1980 by Baker Book House Company

All rights reserved.

Mass market paperback edition issued May 1982 by
Abingdon Press with permission of copyright owner.
ISBN 0-687-15728-5
(previously published by Baker Book House under ISBN 0-8010-4223-2)

To
MY FOREMOTHERS
Ruth Lucille Parr Hardesty
Idella May Swygart Parr (1887–1965)
Jessie Tapscott Hardesty (1874–1934)
Nancy Ellen Peters Swygart Dietz (1859–1939)
Rebecca Rife Parr
Elizabeth Ann Crossley Tapscott (1848–1929)
Sarah Jane Comstock Hardesty (1846–1912)
Cynthia Ann Powell Peters (1822–1858)
Mary A. Swygart
Phoebe Apple Crossley
Maria Rankins Tapscott (1823–1904)
Philena Bond Comstock
Nancy Ellis Hardesty (1818–1884)
Joan Davis Apple
Mary Wright Crossley
Wealthy Tunget Rankins
Anne Schenck Tapscott
Catherine Whippie Bond
Rebecca Copeland Ellis

PREFACE

Therefore, since we have so great a cloud of witnesses surrounding us, let us also lay aside every encumbrance, and the sin which so easily entangles us, and let us run with endurance the race that is set before us (Heb. 12:1, NASV).

● A great cloud of witnesses surrounds us, says the writer of Hebrews, who according to some scholars may have been a woman—Priscilla. That cloud includes not only those believers of our generation who view our race, but also those of past generations.

To use another biblical image, we are all the body of Christ, the church, the communion of saints. In reading about these women, I trust you will be able to empathize with their struggles and triumphs, for I believe these women share in our lives today. They, as part of the body of Christ, witness our race. Having run it themselves, they cheer our beginnings, cringe at our falls, are disappointed by our mistakes, and applaud our victories. Novelist Charles Williams calls it the "coinherence of love." We, with them, are one in Christ.

Many of these short sketches first appeared as a "Capsule" series in *Eternity* magazine (they are reprinted with permission). They have grown out of my own fascination with the diversity and integrity of Christian women, past and present. Women and men throughout history have grappled with the same issues we struggle to understand today: What does it mean to be created in the image of God, male and female, and to live in mutual submission as new creations in Christ? Throughout this book you will find stories of women who have sought to apply Scripture to their lives and to use the gifts God had so manifestly given them.

Some of their experiences may seem foreign, and their expressions of faith quaint to the modern taste. Yet they are our sisters. As we listen to them we can learn, our understanding of God's nature and work can be expanded, and our vision of the race which is set before us can be illumined.

A special word of thanks to John Scanzoni: he always believed that this was a book that should be written. He and Letha Dawson Scanzoni have continually urged me to "keep at it." To them, and to my mother, Ruth Lucille Parr Hardesty, who asked every week, "Is your book done yet?" I say, "This is it. May the God of love and grace be manifest through it."

Nancy A. Hardesty
Epiphany, 1980

EDITOR'S NOTE: The reader may encounter in other sources variants from the spellings of some of the proper names that appear here, particularly those from early times.

CONTENTS

INTRODUCTION

• Church history has been essentially men's history. Libraries contain multivolume sets of the "church *fathers*": Tertullian, Jerome, Ambrose, Augustine, Gregory of Nyssa and of Nazianzus. For the most part, our Christian theology has been shaped by men: Aquinas, Luther, Calvin, Wesley, Barth, Henry, Berkower. And men have shaped our worship: Hippolytus, Cranmer, Zwingli.

At the same time, women have been the life of the church—always a majority of its membership, its worshiping communities, its monastic life, its ministries to others. But within Christianity there has been deep distrust, disdain, and sometimes even dread of women. Take, for example, Tertullian's "You are the devil's gateway," or Aquinas's "Woman is a misbegotten male," or Barth's "Women are ontologically inferior."

The women in this book have felt that pain, that persecution. "Raised consciousness" among women is not only a recent phenomenon. Alert women through the ages have felt the pressures of prejudice. Paula was stung by the criticism Jerome received for allowing women to aid in his translation work. Hroswitha was very aware that poet and playwright were not considered vocations for women. Many made it abundantly clear to Antoinette Brown, Phoebe Palmer, Lydia Sexton, and the host of other women who sought to proclaim the Good News, that public ministry was not a proper activity for women. As mystic and saint, Teresa of Avila once said, "The very thought that I am a woman sometimes makes my wings droop."

Despite being scolded that God did not want their service and that the church did not need it, these women and a mighty army of others persevered. Their contributions to the life of the church are evident to all who carefully read the record of church history.

Women have been told that they are weak and in need of protection. Yet it has often been women's strength and influence which has protected the church. Just as Pope Leo noted of Pulcheria, many women have been defenders of the faith, raised up by God "for such an hour as this" to change, challenge, and watch over the church. Marguerite, Jeanne, and René, along with many others, worked for the Protestant Reformation; Catherine of Siena and Teresa of Avila worked for reform within the church.

Women are particularly evident among the lists of saints of the church—those whose lives and writings have illumined the life of holiness for all of us: Thecla and the Melanias, Elder and Younger, in the early centuries; mystics Catherine of Genoa, Julian of Norwich, Teresa of Avila and Madame Guyon; Methodists Mary Bosanquet Fletcher, Hester Ann Rogers, and Phoebe Palmer; our contemporaries Evelyn Underhill, Simone Weil, Mother Teresa, and Corrie ten Boom. As someone once remarked, women are most visibly included among the saints and martyrs of the church where the only criterion is personal piety. In this they have excelled, and no one could bar their way.

Studies in psychology have shown that, for whatever reason, women do seem to shine in verbal aptitude. This has been evident in the life of the church. Women from Paula (with Jerome) to Anne of Bohemia (with Wycliffe) have encouraged the translation of Scripture. Helen Barrett Montgomery and Ramabai are among those who have made extensive translations of Scripture themselves— a ministry which continues among the many unsung women of the Wycliffe Bible Translators. Women have always been the backbone of Bible and tract societies.

Women have also preached the Word of God—whether they were licensed, ordained, or not. Their eloquence is widely attested; concerning couples such as the Palmers or the Booths, it was often remarked that the woman was the better preacher. Despite intense opposition, Mary Fisher, Antoinette Brown, Maggie Van Cott, Lydia Sexton, Amanda Smith, Clarissa Danforth, and innumerable others have spread the Word of God around the world.

Consistently, they have loved not only in word but also in deed. While women have been theologians—Phoebe Palmer changed entirely the concept of sanctification; Catherine of Siena and Teresa of Avila were named "Doctors of the Church" alongside Aquinas—they have always coupled thought with action. Catherine fed the poor and nursed the sick. Palmer visited the prisons. Missionaries like Ann Hasseltine Judson translated Scripture, and she also wrote grammars and taught people to read. Missionaries Ida Scudder and Clara Swain built medical institutions to heal the sick. They followed in the train of Fabiola, friend of Marcella and Paula, who built hospitals in Rome, and of Catherine, who founded hospitals in Genoa. Florence Nightingale offered to serve the Church of England and was refused; she had to go to Germany to learn nursing. Ramabai's Mukti Mission has become a total haven for women, providing shelter, food, clothing, education, health care, and opportunities to serve others in turn.

Central to all of these women's lives was their love for God, their devotion to Christ, and their compassion for others. Love. Christ commanded that we love God with all our heart. These women did so, often with an intensity and selflessness that affronts us in the post-Freudian, narcissistic twentieth century. We have forgotten how to love God wholeheartedly; we have become fearful of the consequences of such a commitment. As we share their lives, listen to their thoughts, watch their actions, may God rekindle that love in our hearts and lives.

MARCELLA AND PAULA

Bible Specialists

● Women's Bible study groups meeting in elegant suburban homes are not a twentieth-century invention.

Marcella (325–410) gathered one of the first and most influential study groups in her palace on the Aventine in Rome. As a child of the noble and wealthy Marcelli family, she had been impressed by descriptions of Saint Anthony and the men and women who followed him into the Egyptian deserts in order to devote their lives to God. When Marcella was widowed after only seven months of marriage, she decided to serve God by opening her home as a center for Bible study.

One of Marcella's friends was Paula (347–404). Her ancestry, which was claimed could be traced to Agamemnon, included two famous Roman families who gave the empire outstanding generals, orators, and statesmen. At seventeen she married Toxotius of the Julian family (the family tree which bore Julius Caesar), which allegedly descended from Aeneas. Their palace, also on the Aventine, was said to glitter with gold. Paula bore Toxotius four daughters and a son.

When her husband died in 380, Paula was overwhelmed with grief, and her life seemed worthless. "Give Christianity a try," her neighbor Marcella counseled. In the new faith Paula found a reason for living and a new way of life.

Before this the women of the Aventine had devoted themselves to beauty. They dressed in silks and jewels, painted their faces, darkened their eyes, plaited yellow hair pieces into their own dark tresses, wore gold shoes, and were carried everywhere on litters borne by eunuchs. But after they were influenced by Christianity, they forsook the luxury to which wealth entitled them. They adopted plain brown gowns, ate simply, and either rode their own steeds or walked. Their wealth went to charity—blankets to the poor, money and food to the bedridden, burial for paupers. One group member, Fabiola, was inspired to pour her great resources into founding Rome's first hospitals.

Jerome, an eminent church leader, arrived in Rome in 382 to attend a church council, and Marcella asked him to teach her Bible class. He called this class "Ecclesia Domestica," or "the Church of the Household." The leading women of Rome flocked to hear him, and Jerome found them apt pupils.

Of Marcella he declared, "What had come to me as the fruit of language study and constant meditation, she learned and made her own." As one ancient historian commented, she "astonished the holy doctor by her knowledge of the Holy Scriptures, she fatigued him by her thirst always to know more of them than he could teach her; she made him afraid to find in her a judge rather than a disciple."

The class's study was not superficial, nor was it a mere exchange of subjective insights. Jerome was immersed in translating the Bible into Latin, the text we know as the Vulgate. His students learned the original languages (Greek and Hebrew) and served as a "translation committee" to help him wrestle with the most effective presentation of the Word.

After Jerome had returned to Jerusalem, he referred Roman disputes about biblical interpretation to Marcella and declared that even priests sought her as an adviser. Marcella also served as organizer of the local "Bible society," where people could obtain copies of Scripture. Her knowledge of the faith was so astute that when Origen's *On First Principles* was translated into Latin, she immediately read it and pointed out its heretical passages to the pope, who promptly condemned the book.

Her mother wanted her to marry a wealthy senator, but she replied, "Had I a wish to marry, rather than to dedicate myself to perpetual chastity, I should look for a husband and not an inheritance!" In the midst of a very wicked city, she took as her guide Psalm 119:1, "Blessed are those whose way is blameless." With a close friend, Principia, she bought a house farther away from the city where women could retreat to devote themselves to prayer, Bible study, singing of the Psalms in Hebrew, and giving relief to the poor.

When the Goths sacked Rome in 410, Marcella's home was not spared. The invaders burst into her garden and demanded gold. Sure that she must have buried treasure, they beat her; but she died rejoicing that her wealth had all been spent in the service of Christ and that her treasures were laid up where thieves could not break in and steal.

Paula's life was also full of suffering. Not only did her husband die, but two of her daughters died shortly thereafter. When Jerome decided to go to Jerusalem and asked her to go along, she and her daughter Eustochium readily agreed, despite the objections of the two remaining children. They became probably the first Christian women to tour the Holy Land.

Paula was particularly impressed with Bethlehem, and she decided to settle there. She used her enormous wealth to found three convents which she headed, a monastery which Jerome oversaw, a church, and a hospice to shelter pilgrims, orphans, the sick, poor, and elderly.

She served not only as an inspiration and intellectual stimulus to Jerome, but also paid for the books and rare manuscripts he needed. And it was in her convents that the practice of hand-copying the Scriptures was fostered—thus was God's Word preserved for a thousand years until the invention of the printing press.

Jerome would read his translations to her and she would criticize, question, and encourage further research where she found his work faulty. In return he dedicated to her and Eustochium his translations of the books of Job, Isaiah, Samuel, Kings, Esther, Ezekiel, Galatians, Philemon, Titus, and the twelve minor prophets, plus several commentaries.

"There are people," he wrote, "who take offense at seeing your names at the beginning of my works. These people do not know that while Barak trembled, Deborah saved Israel; that Esther delivered from supreme peril the children of God. I passed over in silence Anna and Elizabeth and all other holy women of the Gospel, but humble stars compared with the luminary, Mary. Is it not to women that our Lord appeared after His resurrection? Yes, and the men could then blush for not having sought what women had found."

In 403 Paula's daughter-in-law wrote Jerome to ask how she could rear her tiny daughter, who was named after her grandmother. Jerome outlined a progressive program of education. He suggested giving her tiny boxwood or ivory letters to play with, a stylus and wax to encourage writing, prizes for spelling, and praise to kindle her intellectual excitement.

Teach her Greek and Latin, he advised, and "let her treasures be not silks and gems but manuscripts of the Holy Scriptures," judged not by binding and beauty of calligraphy but by "correctness and accurate punctuation." The young Paula was to be encouraged daily to share the "flowers that she has culled from the Scripture."

Feeling that Rome was too corrupt, Jerome suggested sending her east to live with Paula and Eustochium. She eventually grew in grace and succeeded her grandmother and aunt as head of the convents.

Paula, called "one of the marvels of the Holy Land" by Jerome, died in 440. Six bishops of the church carried her body to its resting place near the birthplace of Jesus.

EMPRESS PULCHERIA

Defender of the Faith

● At the end of the fourth century, the world paused. One era was coming to an end; another had not yet begun. In the Roman world, power was sliding from West to East, and the church was seeking theological balance.

Pulcheria (399–453) was empress in Constantinople when Rome fell. Indeed, she became the only woman to rule the Roman Empire in her own right. Her father was Arcadius, elder son of Theodosius the Great; her mother, Eudoxia, was the daughter of a Frankish general. Arcadius was eighteen and Eudoxia twenty-one at their wedding in 395. Pulcheria was their eldest surviving child. Born on January 19, 399, she was baptized by the famed patriarch of Constantinople, John Chrysostom, the "golden-tongued." Two years later, in April, 401, her brother Theodosius II was born. Two other daughters completed the family of Arcadius and Eudoxia before their untimely deaths.

Theodosius was named emperor of the eastern half of the Roman Empire at age seven, on May 1, 408. The orphaned children were placed under a guardian, but at his death the senate conferred full imperial authority on Pulcheria, as regent for her brother. The title "Augusta" was given to fifteen-year-old Pulcheria with great ceremony on July 4, 414. She took the occasion to make a religious vow of virginity along with her two sisters. She longed to become a deaconess or a nun and retreat to the solitude of Paula's convent in Palestine, but she knew that God had instead given her responsibility for the Empire. Nevertheless she dressed simply, ate frugally, and kept the hours of prayer. In that sense, the palace became her convent. But she also administered the Empire.

Schooled in Latin and Greek, medicine and the natural sciences, theology and law, Pulcheria undertook first to supervise the education of her brother. She found for him a wife in the beautiful Athenais, daughter of the Athenian philosopher Leontius. Educated by her father, Athenais was a good writer, fluent speaker, a master of Greek literature and philosophy.

Pulcheria befriended Athenais, taught her the Christian faith, and stood as her godmother at her baptism in 421. Athenais took as her Christian name Eudocia. On June 7, 421, she and Theodosius were married. Although Empress Eudocia, too, was proclaimed "Augusta" in 423, Pulcheria continued to reign with her brother for another ten years.

During Pulcheria's life, the church so dear to her was plagued with controversy. John Chrysostom had already crossed her mother, Eudoxia, who was offended by his preaching against the extravagances of the court and his comparisons of her with Queen Jezebel. Eudoxia engineered his condemnation at the Council of Chalcedon in 403. An order for his banishment incited riots for days, but a strong earthquake encouraged Eudoxia to repent and have him recalled.

A few months later Eudoxia again turned against Chrysostom when he condemned her construction of a silver statue of herself. This time Chrysostom refused to yield until soldiers slaughtered his congregation of catechumens seeking baptism on Easter Eve

404. When Eudoxia died in labor bringing forth a stillborn child in 405, the people said it was God's judgment. Chrysostom died in 407 on his way to further banishment.

Pulcheria had Chrysostom's body returned to Constantinople on January 27, 438. The Emperor Theodosius knelt beside the tomb and prayed that his parents might be forgiven their persecution of this saint.

He might well have prayed for himself and his own religious choices. Despite Pulcheria's doubts, he appointed Nestorius Patriarch of Constantinople in 428. In the continuing discussion over the definition of Christ's person, Nestorius taught that birth and infanthood were actually unbecoming divinity and thus that Jesus was not fully divine until after his baptism. Nestorius held that at Christ's baptism the divine came to dwell in human form as a spirit within an earthly temple, but the two natures were quite separate and distinct. In the Greek controversy over calling Mary *Theotokos*, "Mother of God," Nestorius suggested that she was *Christotokos*, more than "Mother of man" but somewhat less than "Mother of God." Theodosius's wife Eudocia supported Nestorius.

Nestorius's opponent, Cyril of Alexandria, was supported by Pulcheria. He argued that divine and human natures formed one entity, one person, in Christ from birth. As Gregory of Nazianzus had said, "What is not assumed cannot be redeemed," that is, if Christ had not been fully human as well as fully divine, he could not have redeemed humankind.

The Council of Ephesus in 431 deposed Nestorius as Patriarch and denounced his ideas. Nestorius's followers were so outraged that they attacked the imperial palace and forced Pulcheria to live for a time in suburban seclusion.

Her place as favored counselor to Theodosius was usurped by a eunuch courtier, Chrysaphius. He promoted the cause of his kinsman, an abbot, or *archimandrite* as the Greeks called abbots, named Eutyches, who led many in the Greek church into heresy. Eutyches asserted that Jesus had only one nature; in the union of the incarnation the human was subsumed in the divine. Thus his followers have been called Monophysites (*mono*, one; *phusis*, nature).

Eutyches was condemned by Patriarch Flavian after a trial, and Pope Leo I upheld the ruling. At the urging of Chrysaphius and Dioscorus, the patriarch of Alexandria, Theodosius called the Council of Ephesus, which began on August 8, 449. Pope Leo sent his famous "tome," or statement of faith, defining and defending orthodox Christianity as it had been expounded in Latin terms by Augustine (354–430). But the assembly would not listen to the pope's message. Before a packed house of bishops, Eutyches was absolved and reinstated, Flavian condemned and banished. Imperial troops and mobs of Monophysite priests and monks compelled the bishops to sign the decrees and nearly beat Flavian to death. He died within a few days, but not before he had dictated an anguished appeal to the pope.

When Theodosius ratified the Council's findings, Pope Leo called it "the Robber Council" and appealed to Pulcheria to call an ecumenical council, truly representative of the wider church. At great personal risk, she returned to the imperial palace.

After so many years of suffering and struggle, the tide began to turn in 450. A shaky peace agreement was made with Attila the Hun. Theodosius's horse fell while on a hunting excursion, and Theodosius was mortally wounded. On his deathbed, Theodosius passed over all his advisors and instead named Pulcheria as his successor, a choice unanimously acclaimed by the senate. Pulcheria's coadjutor and protector was to be Marcian, a senator and soldier whom she had chosen. An orthodox Christian who respected her vow of virginity, Marcian became her husband in name only on August 24, 450. Chrysaphius was summarily condemned and executed. The Eutychians were banished, and the followers of Flavian reinstated in their posts.

Pope Leo was pleased. He wrote to Pulcheria:

What we have always presumed concerning the holy mind of your piety, that most fully by experience we have learned that the

Catholic faith though it be assailed by sundry devices of the wicked cannot, while you are at hand raised up by the Lord for its defence, suffer any disturbance. . . . The whole Roman Church exceedingly congratulates you on the works of your faith.

By this time Pulcheria and Marcian had already attended to most of the problems the pope had hoped to solve with a council, but they convened it anyway, knowing themselves just how deep the controversies ran among their subjects. Although papal legates presided, Pulcheria and Marcian set the agenda and drafted the motions. The Fourth Ecumenical Council convened in Nicea, where in 325 the First Ecumenical Council had defined the faith in the great Nicene Creed. Pulcheria wrote the Governor of Bithynia and ordered him to clear the city of all uninvited clerics and monks, lest there be a repeat performance of Ephesus. After the bishops assembled, they moved to Chalcedon. There the great council opened on October 8, 451, and closed sixteen sessions later on November 1. Nearly six hundred bishops attended.

The proceedings of Ephesus were annulled, with many bishops confessing tearfully how they had yielded to coercion. The faith of Flavian was affirmed and Dioscorus was deposed along with his friends. Leo's "tome" was finally read, affirming that in Christ two natures coexist without mixture or confusion, that while they operate separately in principle, they always cooperate.

Between October 17 and 22, the council drew up a creed, based on the Nicene, refuting both Nestorianism and Eutychianism. Its work was ratified on October 25, 451, in the presence of Pulcheria and Marcian, who came expressly to hear it. The Council of Chalcedon declared that the Lord Jesus Christ is

at once complete in Godhead and complete in manhood, truly God and truly man, consisting also of a reasonable soul and body; of one substance [homoousios] with the Father as regards his Godhead, and at the same time of one substance with us as regards his manhood; like us in all respects, apart from sin; as regards his Godhead, begotten of the Father before the ages, but yet as regards his manhood begotten, for us . . . and for our salvation, of Mary the Virgin, the God-bearer [*Theotokos*]; one and the same Christ, Son, Lord, Only-begotten, recognized in two natures, without confusion, without change, without division, without separation; the distinction of natures being in no way annulled by the union, but rather the characteristics of each nature being preserved and coming together to form one person and subsistence, not as parted or separated into two persons, but one and the same Son and Only-begotten God the Word, Lord Jesus Christ; even as the prophets from earliest times spoke of him, and our Lord Jesus Christ himself taught us, and the creed of the Fathers has handed down to us.

Thus the orthodox faith was defined, but sentiments ran deep and factions persisted. Eventually the churches of Persia and India became Nestorian, and those of Syria, Armenia, Ethiopia, and Egypt (the Coptic Church) became Monophysite—but schism between the church East and West was averted for another half-millennium.

Her life work accomplished, Pulcheria died September 11, 453, at the age of 54. She was buried in the Church of the Holy Apostles beside the rest of the House of Theodosius. Her personal estate was given to the poor. Pope Leo called her the "ornament of the Catholic faith," and on her tomb was written: ". . . she preserved her virginity into old age, and wrought many eminent good works in founding churches and hospitals, and in assisting the Fathers of the Holy Synod of Chalcedon; she lies in peace."

HILDA

Ruler with Bishops, Lords, Kings

● By the seventh century, the "civilized" world had been over-run by pagan tribes from the north. Rome had fallen to the barbarians. Social institutions were in disarray.

Yet the light of Christian faith and learning still burned at the far fringes of civilization, treasured and nurtured in monasteries, which were often ruled by women. One of the most famous monasteries was the "Bay of the Lighthouse," *Streaneshalch* as the Anglo-Saxons called it, Whitby as it is known in English. Hilda was its most renowned abbess.

Her story must begin with Clotilda (474–545), queen of the Franks, whose life marks a turning point in European history. Clotilda married Clovis I, king of what is now France, on one condition: that she might continue to practice Christianity.

Her husband agreed, but when their first child died after he had consented to its baptism, Clovis had serious doubts. When a second son became seriously ill after baptism, Clotilda feared her husband's wrath. She took to her knees and prayed for the child, who recovered. When Clovis also was successful in an important battle, he decided that Clotilda's God was more powerful than his own, and so he consented to baptism on Christmas, 496. Clovis was the first major barbarian leader to affiliate himself with Christianity.

Clovis's granddaughter, Bertha, married Ethelbert of Kent in England. Her marriage treaty, like Clotilda's, guaranteed her the freedom to practice her faith, and so she took a personal chaplain with her. Seeing Ethelbert's openness to the gospel, Pope Gregory the Great sent forty monks to England, led by the famous Augustine of Canterbury. Impressed by his wife's witness, Ethelbert soon became a Christian.

Bertha established the first church in England among the Anglo-Saxons. (Christianity was, however, already well-rooted among the Celts of Ireland, and they had established a few outposts such as Iona in Scotland.) Bertha and her original retinue worshiped in a small Roman building outside the walls of Canterbury, but later she and her husband gave Augustine their own home, the site of what is now Canterbury Cathedral.

Their daughter, Ethelberga, married Edwin, King of Northumbria, for whom Edinburgh is named. She too took along her own chaplain, since the Northumbrians still worshiped pagan gods. Edwin, a very thoughtful man, pondered for several years, listening to his wife and to his royal advisers, and finally he decided to accept Christ. Baptized with him on Easter Eve, 627, was his great-niece, Hilda.

Born in 614, just seventeen years after Augustine's arrival, Hilda was of royal blood. When her father was poisoned by a rival, Edwin avenged his death and took the tiny girl home to be educated by Ethelberga. At the age of thirty-three she resolved to devote herself to the religious life.

From 660–80 Hilda was abbess of Whitby, a "double monastery" housing both men and women. In some ways such houses were uniquely Anglo-Saxon, for women of the Germanic tribes were considered equal partners with their men in all the adventures of life. In marriage a couple exchanged arms as well as vows, with the wife receiving horse, shield, spear, and sword. They sometimes rode into battle together. In addition, as the historian Tacitus remarked, Anglo-Saxons believed that "there resides in women an element of holiness and prophecy, so they do not scorn to ask their advice nor lightly disregard their replies."

In the seventh and eighth centuries numerous double monasteries were founded in England, and on the continent under the missionary labors of Willibrord and Boniface. All of them were headed by women. These abbesses possessed considerable power, temporal as well as spiritual. They ruled vast territories. They participated in councils of church and state as equals with bishops, lords, and kings.

Their homes were not the cloistered convents one might picture, but bustling centers of civilization and commerce. Monasteries were the universities of their day, the only places where intellectual and artistic pursuits were undertaken. There books were preserved and copied painstakingly by hand. Monasteries were also centers for evangelistic outreach, spreading the gospel among the surrounding pagans and instructing them in the faith.

One of Hilda's most famous pupils was Caedmon, a simple, pagan herdsman living on the monastery's lands. In the evening around the campfire, his fellows would sing. But Caedmon could not sing, and the other herdsmen would taunt him. One night as he lay among the animals in the stable, he saw a vision of a stranger who commanded him to sing of "the beginning of created things." He insisted he could not, but the stranger persisted. Suddenly the song formed in his mind. Surprised by his sudden talent, his friends took him to Hilda.

Hearing his song, she recognized his gift. To test his powers she explained a short biblical story to him and asked him to put it in verse. By the next day, he had composed a beautiful song. Hilda asked him to move into the monastery proper. Patiently she instructed him in the faith and encouraged him to turn what he learned into ballads. These songs, beloved by his people, inspired many to repentance and faith in Christ. The simple folk could not always understand the Latin of the scholars, but they were caught up by Caedmon's Anglo-Saxon songs. Some have called Caedmon's poetry the precursor of Milton's *Paradise Lost*, and Hilda has been called the mother of English letters.

Hilda instructed the simple and the great. During her administration, five bishops renowned for their holiness and learning went out from Whitby to all parts of England. As the historian Bede says of Hilda, "All who knew her called her mother, on account of her piety and grace." Nobles, bishops, and learned men "did not merely ask her advice, but they also followed it."

The most important event during her tenure as abbess was the Synod of Whitby in 664, which met to discuss differing religious customs. Hilda and King Owsy, who had given lands for the monastery, followed Celtic customs on several matters, including the dating of Easter. Queen Eanfleda and Prince Alchfrid, however, followed Roman practice. As a result, half the court was celebrating Easter while the other half was still commemorating Palm Sunday. The debate at the Synod of Whitby was long and complicated, but eventually Roman customs prevailed. Thus was the English church aligned with more universal Christian practice.

Hilda, described as having a "commanding appearance," and a "great love of God," died on November 17, 680. The great double monasteries which her memory symbolizes survived for another century before they were plundered in Viking raids. They were scarcely rebuilt before being devastated again by the Norman conquerors.

Gradually, as a new medieval society took shape, men's ideas of the proper roles of men and women also changed. The Anglo-Saxon ideas of equality and partnership were forgotten. Men took the places of leadership in the church and women in religious life were increasingly silenced. The golden age of the

English abbesses was forgotten. But as has been said of that period, "The career open to the inmates of convents both in England and on the continent was greater than any other ever thrown open to women in the course of modern European history."

4
LEOBA

Missionary Teacher

● Approaching old age and without children, an eighth-century Englishwoman named Aebba one night dreamed that she was "bearing in her bosom a church bell, which on being drawn out with her hand rang merrily." In the morning she told the dream to an old nurse who said, "We shall yet see a daughter from your womb and it is your duty to consecrate her straightway to God."

Soon that daughter was born to Aebba and her husband Dynno. They named her Thrutgeba, Leoba, which means "beloved." Her parents, members of English nobility, were zealous and God-fearing. As soon as she was grown, they gave her over to the care of Tette, abbess of Wimborne (meaning "wine-stream," named for the sweetness of its water).

It was a double monastery, but there was no crossing between the houses for men and women. Tette, a sister to the king, ruled over both houses "with consummate prudence and discretion." The women were very strictly cloistered from the outside world

—no laymen, clerics or even bishops could visit them. Priests were allowed in only to celebrate the sacraments. Tette dealt with the outside world and with the ruling of the men's house through a small window in the convent.

Leoba was educated in another double monastery, Minster in Thanet, ruled by Abbess Eadburga, daughter of King Centwin of the West Saxons. Leoba became expert in the church fathers, theology, and ecclesiastical law. The Bible was her constant companion—she even had other nuns read it to her as she slept.

Her biographer, Rudolf, a monk at Fulda, who wrote her *Life* about 836, describes her as "angelic" in appearance, "in word pleasant, clear in mind, great in prudence, catholic in faith, most patient in hope, universal in her charity." Her great gifts came to the attention of Boniface, the man who re-formed the church on the continent in the missionary-minded eighth century.

Europe had been in upheaval since the fall of Rome. The decisive battle of Tertry in 687 had given power to the Germanic elements. The vast Merovingian kingdom, covering most of what is now France and Germany, was breaking up, and power was shifting to the Carolingians. The warring tribes were again being woven into a kingdom.

During this time the church had suffered and become disorganized. Bishops had become political pawns of the aristocratic families to which they belonged and the people, lacking instruction, practiced a strange mixture of misunderstood Christianity and pagan customs.

In the sixth century, the continent had been visited by the great Irish missionary Columbanus. Though his mission had been successful at the time, its results soon withered, because it had depended on the charismatic personality of its preachers and had put down no lasting organizational roots.

Boniface, or Wynfred, has been called the "Apostle of Germany." A native of Wessex, in England, his mission was to plant a strong church throughout Germany. He first went to

Utrecht in 716. For the next thirty years, backed by successive popes, he extended the church's reach and gave it an organization tied to the universal church in Rome.

Realizing that a growing church needed a strong monastic life for scholarship and education, Boniface wrote Tette and asked that she send him Leoba, who was the daughter of his friend Dynne and of Aebbe, his kinswoman.

In all, Boniface recruited more than a dozen English monks and nuns to begin monastic life in Germany. Of the twelve named in 748, six were men from Malmesbury and six were women from Wimbourne. Boniface chose as their leaders a man named Sturm, who was to become the first abbot of Fulda, and Leoba, who was to become abbess at Bischofsheim, on the Tauber River in the diocese of Mainz. At Bischofsheim, Leoba trained the women who were to become the superiors of other convents. Says Rudolf, there was "hardly a convent of nuns in that part which had not one of her disciples as abbess."

The eighth century was the zenith of English monasticism, an "intellectual renaissance," in which women played a prominent part. Boniface's letters to women in England are filled with affectionate requests for books, which they copied by hand and sent to him and to the monastic libraries he founded.

Leoba was an outstanding example of this movement. Says Rudolf, "trained from infancy in the rudiments of grammar and the study of the other liberal arts, she tried by constant reflection to attain a perfect knowledge of divine things so that through the combination of her reading with her quick intelligence, by natural gifts and hard work, she became extremely learned."

It was not simply "book learning." Leoba once dreamed that a purple thread was coming out of her mouth. She pulled the thread, and kept winding it into a ball, until she awoke. When she asked an aged nun with the gift of prophecy to interpret her dream, she was told that the thread represented the wise counsels which came from her heart to help others. Because she held it in her hand, that meant that she could put her words into action. The ball of thread signified the mystery of divine truth.

The nun's prophecy proved true, for Leoba was "held in veneration by all who knew her." Even bishops, "because of her wide knowledge of the Scriptures and her prudence in counsel," came to discuss spiritual matters and ecclesiastical discipline with her.

She was also profoundly respected by the Carolingian kings and queens. Charlemagne's wife Queen Hiltigard especially would have liked to have Leoba stay at court and teach. However, reports Rudolf, Leoba fled at once from all the hubbub because she "detested the life at court like poison."

Boniface held her in great affection. Before departing for Frisia in 755, he left special instruction with Abbot Lull and the senior monks of Fulda to take care of Leoba to the end of her life. Seeming to anticipate his own imminent martyrdom, he asked that "after his death her bones should be placed next to his in the tomb, so that they who had served God during their lifetimes with equal sincerity and zeal should await together the day of resurrection." And he gave her his cowl (hooded robe).

Leoba was the only woman ever allowed to enter Fulda, where she would come from time to time to share counsel and to pray. She would leave her entourage nearby and enter the monastery during the day accompanied by one older nun.

When she became too old to govern Bischofsheim, she retired to another convent at Scoranesheim with a band of nuns. There they served God through fasting and prayer.

At her death in 779, she was again taken to Fulda in honor of Boniface's last request. Since the monks hesitated to open his tomb so long after his death, they buried Leoba nearby, beside an altar Boniface had consecrated to Christ and the Twelve Apostles. Together they await Christ's coming.

HROSWITHA

Germany's First Poet, Playwright

● Hroswitha blushed as she read the scandalous plays and poems. Yet even many Christians preferred to read them because of their "finished diction"; this was the only literature available with fine phrasing and poetic construction. Hroswitha vowed that she would proclaim Christian truth in the same beautiful style.

Hroswitha (also known as Hrosvit, Roswitha, or Hrotsvitha, c. 935–c. 1000) was a German woman who in a way owed her spiritual and literary heritage to Hilda, the seventh-century English abbess.

In the eighth century the English missionaries, led by Boniface and Willibrord, took Christianity back to the now-pagan continent. Realizing the need for educational institutions, Boniface petitioned the English abbesses to send members of their double monasteries to help him. As chapter four indicates, it was Leoba his kinswoman who founded and ruled the double monastery at Tauberbischofsheim, noted as a center of learning in Germany. Another recruit was Hygeburg, who wrote the earliest book we know of detailing an Englishman's trip to the Holy Land.

As a young noblewoman seeking an education, Hroswitha entered Gandersheim, another monastery founded by the missionaries, who had furnished its famous, magnificent library. There Hroswitha found many biblical works, as well as the classical writings of Virgil, Lucan, Horace, Ovid, Terence and Plautus.

Many at that time considered the old Roman works unfit reading for a Christian woman, but Hroswitha knew that they embodied the most beautiful usage of the Latin language. Her sisters and superiors encouraged her to use her own considerable talents to turn the classical models into Christian literature. Thus she became Germany's first woman poet and playwright.

Her works, all written in Latin, are of three types. First were her eight narrative religious poems. For the edification of her sisters, she wrote of the Book of Revelation, Christ's ascension, the nativity of the Virgin, and the lives of saints.

"Writing verse appears a difficult and arduous task, especially for one of my sex," Hroswitha admitted in a preface to one of her books. "But trusting to the help of divine grace more than to my own powers, I have fitted the stories of this book to dactylic measures as best I could."

One of her poems, "The Lapse and Conversion of Theophilus," is the earliest attempt in German literature to describe a man making a pact with the devil. Thus, it lays the foundation for Goethe's later use of the Faust legend.

Least important of the three types were her last works, two verse chronicles concerning the reign of Emperor Otto the Great and the history of Gandersheim.

Most important were her six dramas, which were the forerunners of the medieval mystery and miracle plays. Her moralizing comedies copied the prose style of Terence, which occasionally lapses into rhyme and rhythm. His plays concerned the vices and follies of men and women, while Hroswitha's plays dealt with

Christians who met temptation or persecution and emerged victorious through the power of God.

One tells the story of *Dulcitius*, an evil man who had unscrupulous designs on three holy maidens, Agape, Chioma, and Irene. In the end they escaped his machinations through a series of delightful miracles. Another play concerns a lusty young man, *Callimachus*, who pursued the virtuous Drusiana to her tomb, where he met death. Eventually both were raised to life again by St. John and they vowed to live saintly lives. The resemblance of *Romeo and Juliet's* plot to this story has led some to speculate that Shakespeare drew upon Hroswitha's work.

Conscious that her literary vocation was not an ordinary one, Hroswitha begs that readers "not on account of her sex despise the woman who draws these strains from a fragile reed." She knew that some would criticize her creations as inferior to their classical models, but "all I am bent on is, however insufficiently, to turn the power of mind given to me to the use of Him who gave it."

Again in another work she expresses "fear that the abilities that have been implanted in me should be dulled and wasted by neglect; for I prefer that these abilities should in some way ring the divine praises in support of devotion."

Hroswitha struggled between the knowledge of her own talents and her desire for Christ-like humility. In a letter she praised God, through "whose grace alone I have become what I am; and yet I am fearful of appearing greater than I am, being perplexed by two things... the neglect of talents, vouchsafed one by God, and the pretence of talents one has not."

After her death, Hroswitha's writings sank into oblivion for nearly five hundred years before their rediscovery by the Renaissance. At least one of her plays has been translated and produced on the London stage in our own century. The University of Virginia has recently published *Hroswitha of Gandersheim: Her Life, Times and Works*.

Critics through the years have applauded her work. The poetic legends and histories written by the "Nightingale of Gandersheim" ranked highest with her contemporaries, but history has judged her dramatic work as unequaled throughout the Middle Ages.

The keynote of her works is the conflict between Christianity and paganism. Hroswitha drew from the literary heritage of the classical world. But in spirit and essence, her works marked the beginning of that great medieval synthesis of learning and the Christian faith.

CATHERINE OF SIENA

Luther's Predecessor

● Mystics are often viewed by pietists and advocates of social action as hopeless escapists from both reason and action. Yet the true mystic seeks to fulfill the first and second great commandments. Catherine of Siena (1347–80) packed into one short life a deep mystical devotion to Christ and strenuous service to others.

Palm Sunday and the Feast of the Annunciation coincided on March 25, 1347, the day of Catherine's birth. She was the twenty-fifth and last child, the surviving member of a pair of twins, born to a Tuscany dyer. She also survived the plague of 1348, which killed 30,000 people in Siena alone. Clearly she was destined by God for some high purpose.

Inspired by nightly family devotions, Catherine developed a deep love of Christ as a small child and desired to emulate the great saints of the church. At age six she saw her first vision in the sky above her church—Christ the King, seated on his heavenly throne, flanked by Peter, Paul and John, with his hand raised in blessing.

Catherine knew that she should find someplace where she could be alone with God. For a time she would go to pray in a small cave on a nearby hillside. Finally her parents, realizing the seriousness of her religious devotion, gave her a small room in the basement, off her father's shop. With a plank for a bed, a wooden log for a pillow, a small lamp, and a crucifix, she would meditate, fast, and pray in the manner of the desert anchorites.

During her teen years her parents urged Catherine to prepare for marriage, but instead she cut off her hair, vowing to dedicate her life to God. Though they were displeased at first, her parents finally agreed: "May God preserve us, dearest daughter, from trying in any way to set ourselves against the will of God. We have long seen that it was no childish whim of yours, and now we know clearly that it is the Spirit of God that constrains you."

For three years Catherine lived in seclusion and sought God. She learned to find "an inner cell in her soul." On Shrove Tuesday of 1366, while the rest of Siena was caught up in carnival, Christ came to her in what she later described as "spiritual marriage," and placed a ring on her finger. Her soul attained mystical union with God, the goal of all mystics.

Catherine's period of inner growth was complete. She had learned to love God with heart, soul, and mind. Now it was time to love her neighbor. "Do manfully, my daughter," Christ commanded, "and without hesitation those things which will be put into your hand, for now being armed with the fortitude of the Faith, you will happily overcome all your adversaries." She abandoned her solitary cell, returned to the family table and household routine.

Since she was sixteen she had been a Dominican tertiary—that is, one who had taken monastic vows but lived at home. Most other members of the order were elderly widows. For a woman and especially a nun to mix in the city crowds was thought scandalous. Catherine questioned God's leading: "Who am I, a woman, to go into public service?"

"The word impossible belongs not to God; am not I he who

created the human race, who formed both man and woman?" God responded. "I pour out the favor of My Spirit on whom I will. Go forth without fear, in spite of reproach. . . . I have a mission for you to fulfill."

So Catherine began to visit prisons, attend executions to comfort the accused and their families, take food to the destitute, even share her own clothes with the poor. God sustained her work with miracles; a cask of wine lasted three months instead of the one week it should have at the rate she drew pitchersful to share with the sick and needy.

In 1374 the Black Death again swept Siena, killing hundreds daily. With a band of followers, and sustained by her inner sense of the presence of God, Catherine nursed the sick without a touch of revulsion or self-concern.

Yet her own inner piety had given her a physical sensitivity to moral corruption. It was said that upon meeting a person she could instantly sense his inner state by either a sweet savor or a vile odor that made her nauseous.

Devoted as she was to Christ, she began to feel more than a little queasy about the state of his church. Despite the fact that she was a young woman from a very humble background, she set out to reform the church. Long before Luther, she criticized the power of papal legates, the luxuries of the church made possible by the offerings of the poor, the vices that had subverted the monasteries, and the decline of personal piety among the clergy.

The worst scandal was the pope's residence in Avignon. Catherine prayed that the pope would abandon the decadence and dependency of the French court and return to Rome to unify and purify the church. Gregory XI was weak in character, and Catherine, like the prophets of old, did not mince words. She told him that salve was not sufficient for the church's current illness. The wound must be cauterized.

"Do not be a boy, be a man!" she urged. "Since God has given you authority, and you have assumed it, you should use your virtue and power; and if you are not willing to use it, it would be better for you to resign." After much cajoling and many such spine-stiffening lectures, Gregory returned to Rome.

His successor, Urban VI, also sought Catherine's advice and aid in rallying the church. Although she had no diplomatic background and had only learned to read at age twenty, she had great success in bringing the church into line. When several cardinals tried to renounce Urban, she wrote them: "Now you have turned your backs, like poor mean knights; your shadow has made you afraid. . . . What made you do this? The poison of self-love [and] . . . the evil which you have in yourselves."

Her letters to various heads of state were equally blunt. To Queen Joan of Naples she wrote, "Rise up manfully, sweet sister. It is no longer the time for sleep, for time sleeps not, but ever passes like the wind. For love's sake, lift up the standard of the most holy cross in your heart." And to Charles V, who was waging war, she suggested peace: "Now then you will fulfill the will of God and me, and His commands; as I told you I wished to see you observe the holy commands of God."

Catherine died on Easter Sunday, April 29, 1380, in only her thirty-third year. In some ways she had not fully accomplished her goals. Though the church was more united, her call for spiritual purity had been ignored. Churchmen were still too busy with politics. She appealed to the pious hermits living near Rome, but they had refused to become involved, fearing they would lose their own spirituality in the battle to reform the church. Renewal and revival had to wait for another century.

JULIAN OF NORWICH

Trinitarian

● Few have pondered the meaning of the Trinity as extensively as did anchoress and mystic Julian of Norwich in her *Showings* or *Revelations of Divine Love*.

For example, in Chapter 58 of the "long text" (see below) she writes:

> God almighty is our loving Father, and God all wisdom is our loving Mother, with the love and the goodness of the Holy Spirit, which is all one God, one Lord. . . I contemplated the work of all the blessed Trinity. . . . I saw and understood these three properties: the property of the fatherhood, and the property of the motherhood, and the property of the lordship in one God. In our almighty Father we have our protection and our bliss, as regards our natural substance, which is ours by our creation from without beginning; and in the second person, in knowledge and wisdom we have our perfection, as regards our sensuality, our restoration and our salvation, for he is our Mother, brother and saviour; and in our good Lord the Holy Spirit we have our reward and our gift for our living and our labour endlessly surpassing all that we desire in his marvellous courtesy, out of his great plentiful grace. For all

our life consists of three: In the first we have our being, and in the second we have our increasing, and in the third we have our fulfillment. The first is nature, the second is mercy, the third is grace.

Not much is known of Julian at all—in fact, we have no idea what her name was. She is called Julian of Norwich because in later life she lived in an anchorage attached to the church of St. Julian in the English town of Norwich. We do not know if she was a laywoman or a nun.

We do know that she was thirty and a half years old when she fell ill from May 3 to May 8, 1373. She had asked three favors of God: first, a "bodily sight" of Christ's passion that she might share his sufferings as his mother did; second, an illness which would purge, through suffering, her heart and mind from all love of worldly things; and third, three "wounds": of sorrow for sin, of suffering with Christ, and of longing for God.

Her illness brought her to death's door. At that time she was presumably still living at home, for her mother called the local priest to give Julian last rites. As he prayed and lifted the crucifix at the foot of her bed, a light seemed to focus on Christ's face and suddenly all pain left. She realized that there was "red blood trickling down from under the crown, all hot, flowing freely and copiously, a living stream. . . ." During the next twenty-four hours she had a total of sixteen visions. When they were finished, she recovered speedily.

We have two texts of her "revelations," one short, one long. Scholars now believe that she wrote the first one, which contains twenty-five chapters, shortly after May, 1373. Then she became an anchoress in order to meditate on what God had shown her. Twenty years later she wrote the long text, containing eighty-six chapters, to share her reflections on what she had been shown.[1]

---

1. All quotations given here are from *Showings*, edited by Edmund Colledge and James Walsh (New York: Paulist Press, 1978), which contains a modern rendering of both texts.

In later years she became a well-known spiritual counselor and received a number of bequests from grateful friends. She lived at least until 1416.

Although she quite graphically saw Christ on the cross, and at times the Virgin Mary standing alongside, Julian's visions were largely more abstract in nature. God revealed to her (fully in line with Scripture and the church's teaching, she takes pains to point out) the meaning of Christ's suffering, death, and resurrection; the nature of the Trinity; the enormity of God's love and grace to us. In both texts she develops these and a host of other themes, not logically but poetically, most often in trinities of ideas.

Throughout she speaks of the Trinity. In her first vision, she writes, "suddenly the Trinity filled my heart full of the greatest joy, and I understood that it will be so in heaven without end to all who will come there. For the Trinity is God, God is the Trinity. The Trinity is our maker, the Trinity is our protector, the Trinity is our everlasting lover. . . ." She speaks of God as "almighty, all wise, and all good"; and again as "almighty, all wisdom, and all love."

She also describes the operations of the Trinity. In one vision Christ asks her, "Are you well satisfied that I suffered for you?" She answers, "Yes, good Lord," and felt "a joy, a bliss and an endless delight":

> By "joy" I understood that the Father was pleased, and by "bliss" that the Son was honoured, and by "endless delight" the Holy Spirit. The Father is pleased, the Son is honoured, the Holy Spirit takes delight.

Another time she says God "answered to all the questions and doubts" which she raised when he said, "I may make all things well, and I can make all things well, and I shall make all things well, and I will make all things well; and you will see yourself that every kind of thing will be well." She explains:

When he says "I may", I understand this to apply to the Father; and when he says "I can", I understand it for the Son; and when he says "I will", I understand it for the Holy Spirit; and when he says "I shall", I understand it for the unity of the blessed Trinity, three persons and one truth. . . .

And again she declares: "Our Father wills, our Mother works, our good Lord the Holy Spirit confirms."

Some are surprised or shocked to hear Julian speak of Jesus as our Mother, but she is part of a long tradition of medieval spirituality which uses that image. She speaks of Christ as our Mother in two ways: giving birth to us in the labor of the cross, and feeding us, as from a mother's breast, through the elements of Holy Communion. She develops the theme in chapters 57 through 63 of the long text. It flows seemingly from a meditation on Christ as wisdom—the Word, the *logos* of John's Gospel; *sophia*, Lady Wisdom of the book of Proverbs: "the deep wisdom of the Trinity is our Mother."

God the Creator gave us being, but Christ, "our Mother of mercy," "reforms and restores us," through his passion, death, and resurrection. "The mother's service is nearest, readiest and surest: nearest because it is most natural, readiest because it is most loving, and surest because it is truest. No one ever might or could perform this office fully, except only [Christ]."

As "the mother can give her child to suck of her milk," so "our precious Mother Jesus can feed us . . . most courteously and most tenderly, with the blessed sacrament, which is the precious food of true life."

Not only does Christ give us birth and nourish us, but Christ also encourages us to grow:

The kind, loving mother who knows and sees the need of her child guards it very tenderly, as the nature and condition of motherhood will have. And always as the child grows in age and in stature, she acts differently, but she does not change her love. And when it is even older, she allows it to be chastised to destroy its faults, so as to make the child receive virtues and grace. This work, with everything which is lovely and good, our Lord performs. . . .

Throughout her works, Julian's theme is love. It is best summarized by something she saw in her very first vision. She says, God

showed me something small, no bigger than a hazelnut, lying in the palm of my hand, and I perceived that it was as round as any ball. I looked at it and thought: What can this be? And I was given this general answer: It is everything which is made. I was amazed that it could last, for I thought that it was so little that it could suddenly fall into nothing. And I was answered in my understanding: It lasts and always will, because God loves it; and thus everything has being through the love of God.

In this little thing I saw three properties. The first is that God made it, the second is that he loves it, the third is that God preserves it. But what is that to me? It is that God is the Creator and the lover and the protector. For until I am substantially united to him, I can never have love or rest or true happiness; until, that is, I am so attached to him that there can be no created thing between my God and me.

MARGUERITE OF NAVARRE AND JEANNE D'ALBRET

French Reformation Queens

● Germany and Switzerland are usually considered the soil of the Reformation, but it also flowered and flourished in France, nourished by two queens.

Marguerite of Navarre (1492–1549), the sister of Francis I, reported that her mother, Louise of Savoy, always wished to reform the church. Partly because of this godly influence, by the time Marguerite was fifteen, the Spirit of God was manifest in her "eyes, face, walk, speech and in all her actions," according to a sixteenth-century biographer. "She had a heart devoted to God and she loved mightily to compose spiritual songs." Tall, slender, regal, with deep violet eyes, fair complexion and long golden hair, she was married at seventeen to Charles, Duke of Alencon. Though she was not beautiful, she was said to exercise "a strong fascination by her charms of character and intellect."

The seed of reform was planted in her heart by her spiritual adviser Jacques Lefèvre d'Étaples, the "pioneer spirit of the Reformation," one of the founders of the French Huguenot movement. In 1512, some years before Luther's "discovery" of justification by faith, Lefèvre published a commentary on Paul's epistles in which he declared, among other things, that mankind is saved by faith, not works, and that Christ is present in the Eucharist by his own will and not by an act of priestly transubstantiation. In 1523, Lefèvre translated the New Testament into French. Though the theological faculty of the Sorbonne condemned him as a heretic, Marguerite interceded for him and he was acquitted. In the turbulent years which followed, he more than once took refuge in Navarre.

Marguerite also interceded for Louis de Berquin, who was arrested for translating Luther's works after they had been condemned by the Sorbonne. She herself had read Luther's *Babylonian Captivity* and translated into French verse his meditation on the Lord's Prayer. John Calvin and Theodore Beza both studied at the University of Bourges, which flourished under her protection.

After the death of her first husband, Marguerite married Henry d'Albret, King of Navarre. Their castle became a center of religious and cultural ferment. Many Reformers, including Clement Marot, who provided the Huguenot Psalter, held services in the castle basement and Marguerite took communion with them. When Henry discovered this, he broke up the services and struck his wife in anger. She protested to her brother, Francis, who threatened war. Henry begged forgiveness, took instruction from the Reformers himself, and soon became their champion.

Guillaume Briçonnet, Bishop of Meaux, was a friend of Marguerite who also wanted to reform the church. He put a stop to the selling of indulgences, the exhibition of saints' relics and hymns to the Virgin. He curbed monastic abuses, appointed only evangelical pastors, and urged them to recite the creed in the French vernacular.

Marguerite's friendship with Briçonnet, however, went deeper than a common concern for reform. She shared his deeply mystical view of God. The greatest poet of her era, she wrote a cycle of poems based on Psalm 42, with its alternation between "Why art thou cast down, O my soul?" and the answer, "Hope thou in God." Titled *The Mirror of the Sinful Soul*, it was published in 1533. Her reforming ideas were embodied in poems titled "The Primacy of Scripture," "Justification by Faith," and "The Doctrine of Election."[1] Eventually the Sorbonne considered condemning her books as well, but Francis called a halt to their investigation.

A student of Spanish, Italian, German, Latin, Greek, and Hebrew, she surrounded herself with scholars, poets, theologians, composers, and philosophers. (Calvin even rebuked her for her associations with men like François Rabelais, Bonaventure Des Periers, and Étienne Dolet.) She also wrote the *Heptameron*, a collection of medieval society tales. As Will and Ariel Durant have said of her, "In Marguerite the Renaissance and the Reformation were for a moment one."

She carried on a life of action as well. The "prime minister of the poor," she constantly walked among the simple people, listening to their sorrows and attending to their needs. In their tiny mountain kingdom on the Spanish border, she and Henry improved agriculture and commerce, encouraged cloth manufacturing, fostered education, and opened half a dozen hospitals. Her home for orphans was officially titled "Hospice des Enfants de Dieu le Pere," but it soon became known as "Les Enfants Rouges" for the cheery red uniforms the children wore.

Marguerite adopted many of Calvin's teachings, but hoped to reform without splitting the church. Though she sheltered Huguenot leaders, she was frightened by the excesses of the radical masses who desecrated churches and posted scurrilous placards. Her dying words were prophetic: "God, I am well assured, will carry forward the work he has permitted me to commence, and my place will be more than filled by my daughter,

---

1. These are beautifully translated in Roland Bainton's *Women of the Reformation: In France and England* (Boston: Beacon Press, 1975).

who has the energy and moral courage, in which I fear I have been deficient."

Her daughter, Jeanne d'Albret (1528–72), a willful child from birth, was "the very nerve of the Huguenot resistance," to quote Roland Bainton. At fourteen she was committed to a political marriage with the Duke of Clèves. Her mother and uncle ordered her governess to beat her into compliance, but she issued a signed statement proclaiming her resistance and had to be forcibly carried into the church. After the ceremony she escaped Paris and returned to Navarre; the marriage was never consummated. Later and more willingly she married Antoine, Duke of Bourbon and Vendôme, to whom she bore five children, including Henry IV, who signed the Edict of Nantes granting toleration to all Christian groups.

On Christmas Day, 1560, Jeanne boldly proclaimed Calvinism to be the religion of Navarre. Beza, Calvin's successor, was her lifelong mentor, but as she told the Cardinal d'Armagnac, "Your feeble arguments do not dent my tough skull . . . I follow Beza, Calvin and others only in so far as they follow Scripture."

Despite her spunk, her lot was not an easy one. Religious and political wars raged around her. The Huguenots eventually felt they had to go to battle for self-preservation. When their general, Jeanne's brother-in-law, was murdered, she rode out to rally the troops to victory, flanked by her young son and nephew.

Contemporary of both mother and daughter was another French-woman, Renée of Ferrara (1510–75), champion of the Reformation in Italy. When persecution of Protestants became acute even in Navarre, they fled to Renée. She learned her reformed ideas from her English nanny, who read to her from Wycliffe's Bible. Calvin stayed for a month in Ferrara in 1536 before moving on to Geneva.

Renée's spiritual adviser was Morel, an emissary from Calvin. But Morel did not always relish his task. In fact, he sometimes became exasperated with his benefactor. As he wrote Calvin: "Renée wants to attend the meetings of the synod, as does the

Queen of Navarre [Jeanne]. But if Paul thought that women should be silent in church, how much more should they not participate in the making of decisions! How will the Papists and the Anabaptists scoff to see us run by women!" This remark overlooks the fact that had these women not spoken up, the papists would probably have long since burned him, and many other Protestants, at the stake.

EARLY QUAKER WOMEN

Targets of Persecution

● George Fox, founder of the Quakers, said he was concerned "to give women their place and stir them up to take it." He even titled a pamphlet "An Encouragement to All the Women's Meetings in the World." And women certainly responded.

His first convert was Elizabeth Hooton (1598–1672), middle-aged when she first heard Fox, the 22-year-old shoemaker, preach in Nottingham, England, in 1647. She was a member of a local Baptist group, but she found it spiritually dead and worldly. A small band, including Mrs. Hooton, accepted Fox's doctrine and called themselves "Children of the Light." Within three years of her conversion she was imprisoned—first at Derby, then York Castle, Beckenham, and later Lincoln Castle. Her crime was exhorting people to repentance.

Another of Fox's converts was Mary Fisher (1623–98), a Yorkshire servant girl working for a family in Pontefract when Fox preached there in 1651. With her mistress, she began preaching and was soon imprisoned at York Castle for "speaking to a

priest"—her own parish minister! Undaunted by sixteen months
in prison, where she was educated in the faith by other imprisoned Friends, she and another woman set off for the Fen region
where Hooton had been persecuted.

Believing Fox's contention that ministers were not made by
learning ancient languages but by a personal knowledge of Christ
and a gift of the Holy Spirit, she decided to teach knowledge of
the Inner Light to students at Sidney Sussex College—where
Milton and Cromwell had studied. For their efforts the mayor
had the women stripped to the waist and beaten. Their story,
published in a pamphlet titled "The First Persecution," shocked
England, but other persecutions were to follow.

In 1655 when the group began missionary activity abroad,
Mary Fisher embarked for America with a mother of five. But
when they arrived in Boston in May, 1656, they found authorities hostile. A hundred of their books were burned. They
were stripped and searched for marks of witchcraft, and then
thrown into a prison cell. The windows were boarded so they
could not communicate; they would have starved had not someone bribed the jailer. Eventually they were shipped back to England.

In 1657 the intrepid Mary Fisher heard a call to take the gospel
to the sultan of Turkey. "Her experience with the tender mercies
of the righteous [Boston Puritans] may have made the infidel
Turkish terror seem rather faded," one author wryly notes. Arriving in Smyrna, Fisher inquired of the British consul how she
could get in touch with the sultan. Thinking her mission foolish
and dangerous, he put her aboard a ship headed back to England.
She was able, however, to talk the captain into letting her off at
the next port.

Alone in a country where no one spoke her language, she
journeyed six hundred miles on foot overland to find Sultan
Mohammed IV, encamped with his army of 20,000 at Adrianople.
There she announced she had a message from the "great God."
The next day she was received as though she were an ambassador.

All the officers and the government officials were assembled; a translator stood beside her.

When the sultan bade her speak, she paused a moment for prayer. Assuming she was frightened, he encouraged her to speak the word of the Lord to them and not fear "for they had good hearts and could bear it." So she spoke all that the Spirit laid on her heart. When she finished, she asked if he had understood. He replied, "Yes, every word, and it was the truth."

He invited her to stay but when she said that she must return to England, he offered her an escort. She declined, saying that she had safely reached there "without the least hurt or scoff" and God would protect her return journey as well.

She eventually married and returned to America—but not to Boston. She was buried in Charleston, South Carolina.

In 1657, Massachusetts passed a stiffer law against "the cursed sect of Quakers." Anyone who helped them was to be fined. Those caught teaching Quaker doctrines were to be whipped, have their ears cut off and their tongues bored with a hot iron, and be banished if they persisted. In 1658, return from banishment was made a capital offense.

Mary Barrett Dyer and her husband William—as yet devout Puritans—emigrated from London to Boston in 1635. Mary, of good ancestry and independent wealth, was described by a Dutch writer of the time as a woman of "piercing knowledge in many things, fit for great affairs, attractive in stature and countenance and of wonderfully sweet and pleasant conversation." This mother of six gave birth in 1637 to a stillborn child. A dear friend, Anne Hutchinson, was the midwife and tried to keep it a secret. But gossip spread that God was displeased.

Mary stood by Anne during her trial for heresy. When Anne was excommunicated March 22, 1638, Mary walked out of the church with her. The Dyers followed the Hutchinsons to Rhode Island when Anne was banished. It was Mary who gave the funeral address after the Hutchinsons were massacred by Indians in 1643.

In 1652, the Dyers accompanied Roger Williams to England to seek a charter for their new colony. While in England Mary became a Quaker. When she returned to Boston five years later, she was immediately imprisoned. Her husband, who had returned earlier, finally secured her release, promising under oath that she would speak to no one and would not remain in Massachusetts Bay.

In 1659, she journeyed to Boston to visit imprisoned Friends and was promptly arrested. Along with two men she was sentenced to hang on October 27, 1659. They walked to the scaffold hand in hand, praising God—though a drummer was employed to drown their testimonies. Mary watched her two companions die and fully expected to be next. Then she was told that because of her husband's pleas, her life was to be spared. Despite her protests, she was hustled off to Rhode Island again.

Determined to witness to her faith, Dyer returned to Boston the next spring and was again condemned to death. As she mounted the platform on June 1, 1660, her former pastor at Boston's First Church urged her to repent of her errors. She replied: "Nay, I cannot, for in obedience to the will of the Lord God I came, and in his will I abide faithful to the death." Her body lies in an unmarked grave on Boston Commons, but a statue of her stands on the State House lawn.

The Quaker women certainly cannot be accused of being cowardly. In spite of all the Quakers had suffered, Elizabeth Hooton returned to Boston in 1661. The sixty-three-year-old woman was promptly beaten, taken ten miles into the wilderness and abandoned at night. She found her way back to the coast, and took a boat home to England. There she told King Charles Stuart how his subjects in the New World had welcomed her. He signed a warrant giving her the right to buy land in Massachusetts and to build a house to harbor Quakers.

Returning with the king's order, she was again imprisoned, flogged, and starved by the New England Inquisition (as the Quakers dubbed the residents of "the bloody town of Boston").

Eventually she and another elderly woman were tied to a cart and dragged through eleven towns, a journey of eighty miles. In each town they were beaten. Finally they were left in the forest. All in the middle of winter!

Hooton, however, returned to England to live quietly for a couple of years. But when George Fox announced a missionary trip to the West Indies, she could not resist. On January 8, 1672, a week after the party landed in Jamaica, she died and was buried there.

BARBARA HECK

Methodist Pioneer

● Like Abraham and Sarah, Barbara Ruckle Heck (1734–1804) was called to go out from her own country into a new land where she would receive an inheritance from God. She remained faithful to the heavenly vision, and today many worship God because of her.

Barbara was born in 1734 at Ruckle Hill, Balligarrane, County Limerick, Ireland. But she was not Irish—her ancestors were German. In the late seventeenth century, the troops of Louis XIV had devastated the Protestant regions of the Palatinate on the Rhine River. One group fled to County Limerick where they became hardworking yeomen farmers.

At eighteen Barbara professed her faith in Jesus Christ and joined the local congregation. Her German Bible became her textbook and guide. When she was twenty-four, John Wesley came to Ireland. In his *Journals* he reports that after fifty years without pastors who spoke their language, many of the Germans were demoralized, irreligious drunks. But a great number of them listened to his Methodist gospel of salvation and holiness. Barbara was one of them.

In 1760 she married Paul Heck, and the same year they departed for what they hoped would be a better life in America. Accompanying them were Barbara's cousin Philip Embury, his wife, his two brothers, his wife's brother, their families, and several others. They settled in New York City.

Embury was a local preacher and Methodist class leader in Ireland, but other interests claimed his time and energy in his new home. Barbara, a "modest though earnest woman," remained strong in the Lord. In 1765 another group of families arrived from County Limerick, including Paul Ruckle, Barbara's older brother, and Jacob Heck, her brother-in-law.

One day while visiting them, she found the men playing cards. Concerned for their spiritual welfare, she snatched the cards away, threw them into the fire, and warned the men about their sinful habits. Then she went immediately to Philip's home.

"You must preach to us, or we shall all go to hell, and God will require our blood at your hands," she declared.

"How can I preach when I have neither church nor congregation?" he stalled.

"Preach here in your own home and I will gather you a congregation," Barbara quickly replied.

She returned shortly with what was to be one of the first Methodist congregations in America: her black servant Betty, the Heck's hired man John Lawrence, her husband Paul, and herself. Small as it was, the group illustrated the vision of the early church in Galatians 3:28, "There is neither bond nor free, there is neither male nor female: for ye are all one in Christ Jesus."

After leading the group in song and prayer, Embury preached to his small congregation and then enrolled them in a Methodist class meeting. They met weekly thereafter, and soon many of the other German immigrants from Ireland joined them.

Within two years the group had outgrown the Embury home

and a larger room which they had rented. They needed a chapel. Barbara seemed to anticipate the needs of the congregation "with the spirit of a prophetess," as one biographer declares. For some time she had made the enterprise a matter of prayer and from God she had received "with inexpressible sweetness and power," as she described it, the answer: "I the Lord will do it!"

God gave her an architectural design of simple beauty, economy, and utility. The plan was accepted at once by the congregation and they set to work on what is believed to be the first structure built by the Methodist denomination in the Western hemisphere. (John Wesley had been rector of the Church of England's Christ Church in Savannah, Georgia, and George Whitefield had conducted evangelistic meetings during America's first Great Awakening, but no congregations had been established.)

The growing congregation acquired a site on John Street in 1768 and appealed to the citizens of New York for financial help. From the "mayor down to African female servants, known only by their Christian names," 250 people made pledges. Embury himself did much of the carpentry work on the 60' × 42' structure. The exterior was stone, faced with blue plaster. Since dissenters from the established Dutch church were not allowed to build regular churches, the building had a fireplace and chimney like a house. Barbara helped to whitewash the unfinished interior walls and to spread white sand on the bare floor.

Embury constructed his own pulpit and first mounted it on October 30, 1768. His text was from Hosea 10:12, "Sow to yourselves in righteousness, reap in mercy; break up your fallow ground: for it is time to seek the Lord. . . ."

Named the Wesley Chapel, the new building was soon filled with thousands. The seats had no backs, and the gallery was reached by a rude ladder. The singing was congregational—someone began the melody and then all joined in, unaccompanied. Class meetings were held in various homes, and soon the Methodists in England sent a missionary pastor to lead the new congregation. In 1770 they built a parsonage next door, very small but adequate for the needs of the visiting circuit riders—who were usually single.

With the New York City congregation firmly established, the Hecks and Emburys decided to move upstate to Salem in Washington County. There they established another Methodist society, the first in what was to become the substantial Troy Conference. There in 1775, Philip Embury was tragically killed in an unfortunate hay-mowing accident. In due time John Lawrence married Embury's widow.

Again like Abraham and Sarah who found that Haran was not to be their final home, the Hecks and the Lawrences decided to move to Canada at the outbreak of the Revolutionary War. For eleven years they lived in lower Canada, near Montreal. Then in 1785 they journeyed again into the wilderness, to what is now Augusta.

There, in 1785, in the home of the Lawrences, Barbara Heck helped to organize the first Methodist class in Canada. Sam Embury, Philip's son, was its first class leader. The three Heck sons, one of whom was to become an outstanding minister himself, were among the first members. For five years they worshiped together as a community before a circuit riding preacher came to lead them.

Paul died in 1792 at the age of sixty-two, and Barbara, surviving him by twelve years, died in 1804 at the age of seventy. One of her sons found her sitting in her chair with her well-used German Bible open on her lap. Throughout her earthly journeys that Bible had been her constant guide, companion, and comfort.

SALLY PARSONS AND
CLARISSA DANFORTH

Freewill Baptist Preachers

● On that first Easter morning the women were the ones commanded by the angel to tell the good news. The tomb was empty, the Lord was risen and waiting to meet his disciples. Since then many other women have been called upon to bear the same message.

When revival swept the village of Westport, New Hampshire, in 1792, one of those who "experienced religion" was Sally Parsons.

The young teenager immediately ran home to tell her family the good news. Her mother was pleased, but her father became very angry. "If you're going to become one of those fanatical Freewill Baptists, you can just live somewhere else. You're no longer welcome here!" he shouted.

With tears in her eyes, Sally walked to the door. Outside she knelt and prayed that God would forgive her father and change his heart. She also asked the Lord to protect and encourage her mother, brothers, and sisters. Then she went to stay with a kindly neighbor family.

Despite the difficulties of her life—or perhaps because of them—Sally's faith grew strong. She knew that God was calling her to travel and tell other people about Christ's love for them. She began preaching on the New England frontier wherever she could gather people to hear the gospel.

In 1797, the New Hampshire Yearly Meeting of the Freewill Baptists took notice of the good work Parsons was doing. "But she could travel so much farther and easier if she had a good horse," one member suggested. The rest agreed, and voted to equip Sally Parsons with a horse, a saddle, and a bridle "so long as she should see her way clear to travel and labor in the cause, by exhortation, prayer and personal effort."

For the next four years she preached up and down the state. Even her family began to realize how genuine her faith was and what outstanding gifts God had given her. One by one they became true Christians—even her father. Apologizing for barring her from the house, he asked her forgiveness and promised her a dowry if she should decide to marry.

Eventually she did marry Benjamin Walton Randall, another minister among the Freewill Baptists. As a wedding gift and in recognition of their mutual ministry, the Yearly Meeting relinquished all future claim on the horse.

Another Freewill Baptist preacher was Clarissa Danforth. She was "a lofty, vain young lady" of seventeen in 1809 when she decided to commit her life to Jesus Christ. Soon she became an active Christian. At that time women were seldom preachers, except among the Quakers. In fact, women were generally forbidden to speak, pray, or preach in any religious meeting attended by both men and women.

Sometimes, however, women could speak up at "social meetings," which Clarissa began to do. People were so impressed with her gift for explaining Scripture that they began to schedule "social meetings" just so she could share her insights. Eventually it became more and more clear that God was calling her to be an evangelist. She made her debut as a preacher in 1814.

"A young lady of respectable parentage, good education, extraordinary talents and undoubted piety," she is described by one biographer as "tall in person, dignified in appearance, easy in manners, with all elements of a noble woman." As a speaker, "her language was ready and flowing, her gestures few and appropriate, and her articulation so remarkably clear and full, that she was distinctly heard in all parts of the largest house."

I. D. Stewart, a Freewill Baptist historian, declares that she was the "sensation preacher of the decade" from 1810–20. "Her clear articulation, strong voice, command of language, self-possession, deep piety, and good common sense, rendered her an effective speaker; and whoever could divest himself of prejudice against a woman's appearance in public, listened to her preaching with profit as well as delight."

She held meetings throughout her home state of Vermont, as well as in New Hampshire and western Massachusetts. In October, 1818, she preached her first sermon in Burrillville, Rhode Island. She spent most of her time for the next few years in that state, which resulted in many revivals and the organization of several new churches. She spoke not just among the Baptists, but "almost all the houses of worship in that region were opened to her, and ministers and people in multitudes flocked to hear, and listened with deep emotion." A revival she began in July, 1819, at Smithfield continued for sixteen months!

In December, 1820, Clarissa returned to her hometown of Weathersfield, Vermont, where she remained for the next six months. During that time no less than a hundred people were converted to the cause of Christ. Eventually she married "a gentleman of fortune in Connecticut," and they moved to eastern New York. But even with a family she continued her ministry as she was able.

In the case of Sally Parsons and Clarissa Danforth the stone of prejudice against women's ministry was rolled aside, and through their work the risen Lord was made manifest to many.

ISABELLA GRAHAM AND
JOANNA BETHUNE

Sunday School Pioneers

● "My dear wife, there is no use in waiting for the men; do you gather a few ladies of different denominations and begin the work yourselves!"

Acting upon this advice, Joanna Graham Bethune (1770–1860) organized the first society for the promotion of modern Sunday schools in America. The purpose of the original schools was not, as is so often the case today, to nurture the children of middle-class church members, but to educate and evangelize the poor of all ages.

Joanna was the second daughter of John and Isabella Graham (1742–1814). John Graham was a widower with two sons when he married Isabella. A British army surgeon, he was assigned to Fort Niagara, New York, when Joanna was born February 1, 1770. As revolution drew near, he was transferred to Antigua, where he died in 1773. Isabella, pregnant with another son, returned home to Scotland. There Joanna's childhood friends included

"Waltie" Scott, later more well known as Sir Walter. Isabella supported the family by teaching primary school.

In 1789, the family immigrated to New York City, where Isabella soon became involved in many educational and charitable activities in addition to her teaching. In 1797, she helped found the Society for the Relief of Poor Widows with Small Children, later known as the New York Orphan Asylum. It was the first of many such benevolent societies.

Isabella kept in touch with friends in Scotland, and often gathered her new neighbors in America to hear the latest sermon, tract or news of revival from the old country. During a visit there, she learned of the Edinburgh Gratis Sabbath-School Society. Aided by her daughter, Joanna, she began a class on Mulberry Street in 1792 primarily to teach poor adults to read.

In 1794, Joanna experienced a deep religious conversion, of which she remarked, "From that moment all was rapture." A year later she married Divie Bethune, another Scottish immigrant with a very successful import-export business. A devout Christian himself and involved in many worthy enterprises, he was a liberal supporter of the work of his wife and mother-in-law. During a business trip to England in 1801–02 the couple further familiarized themselves with various types of Sabbath schools being developed.

After they returned home, Joanna and Isabella started a Sunday school in the fall of 1803 in the home of a Mrs. Leech. They personally financed this and two later schools for poor children. During their summer travels upstate they encouraged other women to found similar schools. In 1814, shortly before Isabella's death, they began another school for "ignorant" adults in Greenwich. "The Sabbath previous to her last sickness occupied her with [this] recent institution," according to a eulogy given on August 14, 1814, by the Rev. J. M. Mason.

Sabbath schools, primarily for the education and religious instruction of poor children who either worked in the factories or could not afford private schooling, were being formed in several cities. As early as 1804 the women of various denominations had formed a union society for the education of poor female children in Philadelphia. In a day when the sphere of women was almost totally confined to the home, twenty-six members of the society applied to the state in 1808 for incorporation. In a precedent-setting decision, the superior court decreed that women were indeed "citizens of this commonwealth" and thus entitled to file such a request. Their curriculum included reading, writing, sewing, Scripture memorization, hymns and catechism.

For many years churches and clergy adamantly opposed Sunday schools. They charged that it was Sabbath-breaking to teach or study on Sunday, that such schools usurped the rights of parents and local churches, that interdenominational cooperation was dangerous, and that church buildings should not be used for the general education of non-members. There was also a certain mistrust of the "ignorant and generally vicious" poor.

But the backing of devout, determined women sometimes overcame prejudice and sometimes took advantage of it. In 1815 Mrs. Ann Rhees wanted to start a school at the First Baptist Church in Philadelphia. Pastor Holcombe had little faith in the project, but consented: "Well, my sisters, you can but try it; blossoms are sweet and beautiful, even if they produce no fruit." The deacons of Medway, Massachusetts, were more alarmed: "These women will be in the pulpit next!"

About 1812 the Bethunes began to learn from British friends about a new type of school being developed by Robert Raikes and his followers. They received newspaper articles, books, and brochures describing the new system. Excitedly, they shared them with acquaintances in New York and Philadelphia. The men discussed the project at length and vowed to start an American society, but time wore on and nothing happened.

In a letter to friends in Bristol, England, Joanna wrote that Divie had published some material from England in the local paper and she had lent different publications to a number of friends "in hopes the gentlemen would come forward in the business, but after waiting a number of weeks, I conversed with several of my own sex, who expressed a wish to unite with me in a Female Sunday-School Union."

Accordingly, she called a meeting for January 24, 1816, at a lecture room of the Wall Street Church. Several hundred women attended. After the pastor had opened with an appropriate prayer and had withdrawn, Mrs. Bethune took the rostrum. She impressed upon them "the great need of such an institution in a city where numbers of one sex were training for the gallows and state prison, and of the other for prostitution." She then read extracts from British publications until "there was not a dry eye in the room, and tears flowed copiously down the cheeks of many." She recruited subscriptions and volunteers from various denominations to meet at her home to draw up a constitution, which they presented at a second general meeting a week later.

A Presbyterian herself, Mrs. Bethune was joined by Mrs. Francis Hall, a Methodist; Mrs. William Colgate, a Baptist; and Miss Ball, a member of the Dutch Reformed church. Using the constitution of the Bristol society, they organized "The Female Union for the Promotion of Sabbath Schools," the first such organization in the U. S. to establish schools on the voluntary plan. Their stated purpose was "to stimulate and encourage those engaged in the education and religious instruction of the ignorant; to improve the methods of instruction; to promote the opening of new schools; to unite, in Christian love, persons of various denominations engaged in the same honorable employment." Mrs. Bethune was elected first directress.

They agreed to begin schools a week and a half later, but some were so eager that they began three schools the next Sunday. Mrs. Bethune had launched a new class for black adults the week before. These four original classes had 136 scholars, but by the second Sunday of February the women were teaching a thousand people. By July there were two hundred fifty teachers and over three thousand pupils. Within six years there were six hundred teachers in the city, around seven thousand students, and at least thirty graduates of the classes were training for the ministry.

Of course, by this time the men had gotten organized to teach members of their own sex. In 1817, the Bethunes were instrumental in the founding of the American Sunday School Union, of which the Female Society eventually became an auxiliary, giving women leaders of the local organizations an extremely rare privilege of representing their group at a national religious gathering (though some female societies deferred to custom and sent male representatives—with their offerings).

Seeing the country expanding westward, the A.S.S.U. became the keystone of a national evangelization campaign, along with the American Education, Home Missions, Bible and Tract societies. First in 1830 they launched the "Valley Campaign" to saturate the Mississippi Valley with the gospel. This was so successful that within four years they undertook the "Southern Enterprise" to reach the coast from Maryland southward. In 1835 they began to send workers around the world.

Though women were often, then as now, ignored in the policy-making process for such campaigns, their financial help and their work in the field were essential. Women teachers were always the backbone of the voluntary system. In frontier communities, even before the organized church arrived, a group of women often superintended and taught Sunday schools for their children.

Mrs. Bethune taught her own classes until she was past eighty. For thirty years she taught in the tough Five Points district of New York City. Always interested in primary school education "as a science as well as a charity," she established a society for the advancement of the innovative methods of Pestalozzi, a forerunner of Montesori. She also wrote several books on toddler school instruction.

In a time when "a married woman had hardly more legal status than another article of household furniture," as one historian describes it, the work of such women as Isabella Graham and Joanna Bethune was indeed an example of Christian initiative and discipleship.

LYDIA SEXTON

Mother in Israel

● Lydia Sexton (1799–1873) knew that her call to preach came from God, but she wrestled with it for ten years. After all, she was a wife and a mother, middle-aged and with a family to raise on the Midwestern frontier. As she says in her autobiography, most of all Lydia Sexton was beset by a "man-fearing spirit."

She had been born April 12, 1799, in Rockport, New Jersey, to a Hard-Shell Baptist preacher named Thomas Casad and his wife, Abigail Tingley Casad. They believed that "women should keep silence in the churches"—though Abigail often sang so clearly it was said she could be understood a half mile away. When Lydia was a child, her father died. Her mother wished to remarry another preacher who already had a family of his own, and the Casad children were distributed to various relatives.

At age twenty, Lydia married Isaac Cox, two years her junior. Their first child, John Thomas, was born February 7, 1821, in Fairfield, Ohio. A year later Isaac went to seek work in Indiana, where he was severely injured in a fall. He died in November, 1822.

When the child was three, Lydia gave him to a Dutch family named Kurtz, who were wealthy but childless. She visited him each Sunday when she could.

In 1824 Lydia married again. Moses Moore was an educated man, a United States surveyor who had traveled extensively. He became a school principal in Middletown, Ohio. Their son, Finley Moore, was born January 28, 1825. Within eight months the family again met tragedy—Moses Moore died. Lydia taught for three months to fill out his term. She then reclaimed her first son John, who had been crippled by an accidentally severed Achilles tendon. His head was full of lice and his language was a jumbled mix of Dutch and English. But at least the family was together.

Lydia then met Joseph Sexton. He was a twenty-two-year-old blacksmith who played the fiddle and danced well. Though he was eight years her junior, they were finally married on September 12, 1829; she was to live with him for fifty years. Together they had three more sons, Thomas, Zadok, and David. And they moved with the frontier—from Ohio, to Indiana, to Illinois, and finally to Kansas.

Convicted by remembrances of her own early family home, she began to take an interest in religion. With a seeking heart, she went to a "New-Light" meeting and foot-washing service in the neighborhood. She wanted to go to the altar, but she was afraid of her mother-in-law's reaction. She went to visit a nearby pastor but while she yearned to talk of spiritual things, he discussed politics and pork prices with her husband. Finally she sought out a devout woman named Rachel Nicholas, who told her what she must do to be saved. With Rachel's instruction, Lydia experienced the glorious relief of conversion.

She went to a "Campbellite" meeting to see her brother and cousin baptized in the Great Miami River at Dayton—and she came away baptized herself. She considered joining this group but finally decided not to "if the main feature of their religion was to make fun of the Holy Ghost and the Methodists."

Wanting to remain true to her Baptist heritage, but finding no church to join, Lydia considered trying to live as a Christian outside the church. Finally she visited a meeting of the United Brethren Church in Germantown, Ohio. And as she says, "Although I had not a relation on earth that would join the church with me, I soon found fostering fathers and nursing mothers there." It was to become her church home.

After hearing her speak at a love-feast, an elder in the church offered her a preaching license at once. Thus began a long struggle with her call. She refused the license, though she continued to preach. After a year of preaching she was again offered a license and again she refused. Finally, in 1851, her class meeting took the matter into its own hands and voted to license her. They presented their decision to the quarterly meeting of the United Brethren Illinois Conference, and she was licensed—the first woman to be so licensed by the Brethren. (This makes her the first woman to be officially licensed to preach by the United Methodist Church, long antedating the 1869 licensing of Maggie Newton Van Cott.)

After renewing her license quarterly from 1851–58, Lydia asked that it be made an annual license, saving her a great deal of travel in renewing it. The General Conference, however, had decided to license no woman, for fear that they would ask to be elders and even bishops! Yet they could not deny Sexton's gifts and the validity of her ministry, so they "recommended" her as a preacher *for life* and gave her "credentials" as an approved "pulpit speaker" and a "useful helper in the work of Christ."

Later she notes that her only opposition was from among preachers "of the male persuasion," "who appeared to feel their consequence as male preachers." She often worked as a tailor to support herself, and noted that a women would be paid three dollars for a coat while a male tailor would receive seven dollars for the same work. She observed "that whenever it can be done, even down to the matter of needle-work, men are inclined to monopolize all branches of labor, as well as the professions. Aye, even into the kitchen they come, and immediately demand and receive double wages."

Despite her own struggles, Lydia always encouraged other women to follow the same path. She spoke often of sisters whom she believed were called to ministry and prayed that God might give them "the victory over the man-fearing or man-pleasing spirit."

She continued to preach and travel, sometimes leaving her children at home with her husband. When in 1855 her son Thomas died while she was away on a preaching trip, some neighbors were critical, but Sexton replied that she had always felt that her call was from God and that she must trust her children's lives to God. Staying with them every moment was no guarantee that accident and illness would not befall them. In later years her husband traveled with her, supporting her work.

At age seventy, when most people's life work is complete, Sexton moved to Spring Hill, Kansas, in 1869. There she was asked to be the first woman prison chaplain at Kansas State Prison. By that November she had developed a class system using inmates, including two "exhorters," four class leaders, and had five studying for the ministry. And that from a congregation which numbered only twenty in April! Though she resigned a year later, she continued to preach and minister there until her death, baptizing and giving communion to a class that eventually numbered nearly one hundred.

One author has suggested that "Lydia Sexton's life reads like soap opera." That it does. But despite all the obstacles and opportunities, she is one of whom Jesus would say, "She hath done what she could and wherever the gospel is preached what she has done will be told in remembrance of her."

SARAH DOREMUS

"Mother of Missions"

● At its founding, the missionary enterprise in America was "for men only." The first missionary society was founded in 1795 by William Carey. Soon many other organizations sprang up to evangelize frontier settlements, the Indians, and the "overseas heathen."

Excluded as members by the male missionary organizations, in October 1800, the Baptist and Congregational women of Boston established the Female Society for Missionary Purposes. Its organizer was Miss Mary Webb, an invalid confined to a wheelchair, who spearheaded a movement which soon spread throughout New England and down to New York, Pennsylvania, and west to Ohio. Their goal was "diffusion of gospel light among the shades of darkness and superstition." All of the societies united in prayer the first Monday of each month. Dues were two dollars annually.

But not all women could spare that much from their household budgets. In 1802, Mrs. Mehitable Simpkins founded the Cent

Society. Women were to contribute one cent per week. According to an ad placed by Mrs. Simpkins in the *Massachusetts Missionary Magazine,* the money was "to procure Bibles, Dr. Watts' Psalms and Hymns, Primers, Catechisms, Divine Songs, Tokens for Children, etc." Methodist women called their groups "Female Mite Societies." Others were labeled "Pious Female Praying Societies." They largely supported work among the American Indians.

In 1810, the missionary thrust turned outward, with the founding of the American Board of Commissioners for Foreign Missions. Though this was another all-male society, its first major gift came in the form of a bequest from Sally Thomas, a domestic servant in Cornish, New Hampshire. Though she never received more than fifty cents per week for her work, during a long and industrious life she managed to save $345.38. The Board's first large bequest came from Mrs. Mary Norris of Salem, Massachusetts, who donated thirty thousand dollars at her death in 1811.

As missions historian R. Pierce Beaver declares in *All Loves Excelling,* "American women rallied to the new cause of overseas missions with enthusiasm. In it they would soon find a role of ministry and status denied them in the churches in the homeland." The first woman to apply for an overseas appointment was a widow, Charlotte H. White, who applied in 1815 to the Baptist Board of Foreign Missions. She offered to pay her own way and to live as the sister of Mrs. George H. Hough. Mr. Hough was an ordained minister and a printer. (Such living arrangements were often decreed by mission boards but left nationals with the impression that Americans were polygamous!)

Arriving in Calcutta, however, Mrs. White met and married Joshua Rowe, a British missionary. Flexible and visionary in some areas, Adoniram Judson was glad for the marriage: "We do not apprehend that the mission of single females to such a country as Burma, is at all advisable. . . . In regard to the instruction of native women and children, we apprehend, that if every missionary is married, as he ought to be, these departments will be adequately supplied."

Missions insisted that male candidates marry so that wives could set an example for new converts. In addition, some countries' customs allowed only women to properly teach other women and children. To Board officials, wives were secondary and subordinate, but to laywomen at home they became heroines. Voluminous correspondence resulted. Although wives were given no official recognition by mission boards, they were expected to assume the dual responsibilities of home and ministry. In lands where climate and hygiene were taxing, many women fell under the burden. Judson buried three wives; one patriarch in China lies flanked by seven!

Yet it was considered highly improper for women unencumbered by families to serve (St. Paul's advice notwithstanding). The first single women were allowed to go no further than the American Indians—which was actually a far more rigorous assignment than many overseas. The first unmarried foreign "missionary" was Betsey Stockton, a black woman who went to the Sandwich Islands in 1823. Born a slave in Princeton, New Jersey, about 1798, she served in the home of Princeton's president and read in his library. She applied independently to the mission board, but she was assigned as a domestic assistant to the family of Charles S. Stewart. On the field she put her education to good use; she ran a school for two years, until Mrs. Stewart's health failed and the group returned home.

The first single woman actually given the designation of missionary was Cynthia Farrar, who in 1827 sailed to Marathi Mission in Bombay, after people there pleaded for a woman to head a school. They asked that she not be a wife but someone who could devote full time to the work.

Farrar was born in Marlborough, New Hampshire, in 1795. She professed her faith and joined the Congregational Church in 1815. During her thirty-four years of service to the mission, she gained high praise from churchmen and British officials.

When the semicentennial of American overseas missions was celebrated in 1860, there were five major mission boards and five minor ones. Only thirty single women had been allowed to serve abroad. By 1900 there were ninety-four sending agencies and forty-three supporting ones. Of these, forty-one were women's boards. Major impetus came from the women's rights movement and its promotion of women's education.

The "Mother of Missions," and the driving force behind mission organization, was Sarah Platt Haines Doremus (1802–77), a member of the Reformed Church in New York City. Her husband was Thomas Doremus, a man of wealth and influence who encouraged her work. Mother of eight daughters, one son, and several adopted children, she still found time to teach an infants' Sunday school class, aid Greeks harrassed by the Turks, promote the Grande Ligne Mission in Canada, serve in the women's ward at New York's infamous "Tombs" prison, form the Women's Prison Association to work with discharged prisoners, manage the City and Tract Society to evangelize the poor, help the Bible Society distribute Scripture, organize the Presbyterian Home for Aged Women, found the School of Industry and the Nursery and Child's Hospital.

A physician had a plan to found the Women's Hospital of New York State. He had gained the endorsement of three hundred physicians and many prominent women, but couldn't get the project off the ground. He went to Mrs. Doremus and within six days she had a board functioning. Then she set off for Albany to secure a charter and a ten-thousand-dollar state appropriation!

She had always been interested in missions as well as local philanthropy. Once her husband gave her an expensive shawl, but she asked if she could return it. With the refund she bought embroidery materials and eventually the finished projects netted five hundred dollars for the work in Hawaii.

In 1834, she met David Abeel, a missionary of the Reformed Church of America. He was returning from service in China with a plea from women there: "Are there no females who can come to teach us?" In London he had founded a Society for Promoting Female Education in the East and he hoped to do the same in New York. Mrs. Doremus was enthusiastic, but their plans were scuttled by officials of the American Board.

Mrs. Doremus's heart was stirred again by the pleas of Mrs. Francis Mason, who returned to America in 1860 from her work educating women in Burma. She wanted to recruit single women to help her, but the Baptist Board rebuffed her request. She turned to Mrs. Doremus and within months the first inter-denominational mission agency was formed.

As the first president of the Women's Union Missionary Society of America for Heathen Lands, Mrs. Doremus made her home the society's headquarters. Its first missionary was Sarah H. Marston, who sailed in November, 1861, for Toungoo, Burma. Within a decade the society had missionaries in India, China, Syria, Greece, and Japan. Soon denominations also formed women's missionary boards. But men never did trust such groups. One pastor explained to Mrs. Doremus that he made it a point to attend all of their prayer meetings because "You never can tell what women may take to praying about if left alone!"

A woman of vast talents, Mrs. Doremus not only had administrative skills but was also willing to work on a very menial level. Often she would go to the markets early in the morning to carefully buy items—not only for her own family, but also for hospitals and resident missionaries. Her home was a hostel for departing and returning missionaries as well as a sanitarium for ailing ones. She entertained lavishly—she once had two hundred ministers and their wives in to honor a missionary bishop and twelve of his colaborers from China. "With exquisite courtesy, tact and good humor," Mrs. Doremus was a consummate fund raiser—if a person said he was not interested in foreign missions, she would instead pull out a proposal for some home mission or philanthropic work.

As Helen Barrett Montgomery notes, "Perfectly consecrated to Christ's service, she yielded her life into His control, and the fullness of His power flowed through her life unhindered. A heart at leisure from itself to soothe and sympathize was hers. Her powers were not frittered, but directed."

PHOEBE PALMER

Holiness Unto the Lord

● "Does not every woman that opens her mouth in the church in the presence of a man, to sing or to cough, or, if fainting, to say, I am ill, render herself liable, on this principle, to be silenced? In either of these she breaks silence."

Although Phoebe Palmer disavowed any intention of discussing "the question of 'Women's Rights' or of 'Women's Preaching,' technically so called," she could not restrain her sarcasm at the thought of men commanding women's silence in the church.

Out of compassion for her sisters suffering under such prohibitions, she wrote a book titled *Promise of the Father* in 1859. She pointed out that the prophet Joel had recorded God's promise, "I will pour out my spirit upon all flesh; and your sons and your daughters shall prophesy" (Joel 2:28). It was to this that Jesus alluded when he told the disciples, "Behold, I send the promise of my Father upon you: but tarry ye in the city of Jerusalem, until ye be endued with power from on high" (Luke 24:49). On Pentecost "cloven tongues like as of fire" sat on the heads of the hundred and twenty assembled in the upper room, including "the women, and Mary the mother of Jesus" (Acts 2:3; 1:14–15). "And they were all filled with the Holy Ghost, and began to speak. . . ." (Acts 2:4).

Suppose, said Palmer, that one of these first century "brethren" later came upon a sister proclaiming Jesus to a group of people. "And now imagine he interferes and withstands her testimony by questioning whether women have a right to testify of Christ before a mixed assembly. Would not such an interference look worse than unmanly?" Palmer went on to ask,

> And were her testimony, through this interference, restrained, or rendered less effectual, would it not, in the eye of the Head of the church, involve guilt? Yet we do not say but a person may err after the same similitude and be sincere, on the same principle that Saul was sincere when he withstood the proclamation of the gospel, and made such cruel havoc of the church. He verily thought he was doing God service. But when his mind was enlightened to see that, in persecuting these men and women, he was withstanding God, and rejecting the divinely-ordained instrumentalities by which the world was to be saved, he could not longer have been sincere unless he had taken every possible pains to make his refutal of error as far reaching as had been his wrong.

Palmer was defending not only the ministry of her sisters but also her own. Without asking for ordination or even a Methodist preaching license, Palmer and her husband Dr. Walter Palmer traveled throughout the eastern U. S. and Canada. They also spent four years extending the "holiness" or "lay" revival of 1857–58 to the British Isles. One eulogist says that in all, twenty-five thousand souls were saved under her instrumentality. Countless more experienced "entire sanctification."

Palmer might well be called the "Mother of the Holiness Movement," which eventually gave birth to such denominations as the Church of the Nazarene, the Church of God (Anderson, Indiana), the Salvation Army, and also Pentecostal groups like the Assemblies of God, the Pentecostal-Holiness Church, and the Church of God (Cleveland, Tennessee).

She was born on December 18, 1807, the fourth of ten children of American Methodist Dorothea Wade and Englishman Henry Worrall, who had been converted under John Wesley's ministry. On September 28, 1827, Phoebe married Walter Palmer. Both were lifelong New Yorkers.

Within three years the Palmers lost two baby sons. A third child, Sarah, survived to become a Methodist minister's wife, but another daughter Eliza was burned to death at eleven months when a nurse accidentally touched a candle to netting over her cradle. A third daughter, Phoebe, married publisher Joseph Knapp, and is best remembered as composer of the music for her mother's hymn "The Cleansing Wave" and Fanny Crosby's "Blessed Assurance." Their last son, Walter, Jr., became the publisher for his parents' writing ventures.

Palmer somehow found time to distribute tracts in the slums and regularly visit the Tombs, the notorious New York prison. With backing from the Methodist Ladies' Home Missionary Society, she founded the Five Points Mission in 1850, a forerunner of later settlement houses.

Phoebe's sister, Sarah Worrall Lankford (1806–1896; she became the second Mrs. Walter Palmer in 1876), experienced "entire sanctification" on May 21, 1835. Though the experience was one testified to by many early Methodists in response to John Wesley's teachings on "Christian perfection," it had not been stressed as much by Americans. In August, 1835, Sarah founded the Tuesday Meeting for the Promotion of Holiness, which met in the home the Lankfords and Palmers shared. They met there even when crowds numbered more than two hundred. The Tuesday Meeting, catalyst for a movement which changed the shape of American Protestantism, continued for sixty years.

Phoebe claimed her sanctification on July 26, 1837. As she studied the Bible, Wesley, and the writings of her contem-

poraries such as Oberlin College professors Charles Finney and
Asa Mahan, she came to a new understanding of Christian perfection, or "holiness." In response to a Presbyterian minister's
question whether "there is not a *shorter way* of getting into the
way of holiness," she wrote *The Way of Holiness* in 1846.

She began with the premise that "God requires *present* holiness." Using Finney's logic, asserting that God would not command something people are unable to do, Palmer declared that a
person must first consecrate everything to God. (Volumes of
subsequent testimonies showed this to usually include one's children, spouse, material possessions and reputation; for women it
often included being willing to preach.) Using rather dubious
biblical exegesis, Palmer termed this "laying all upon the altar."
She declared that the altar is Christ and that "whatever *touched*
the altar became holy, virtually the *Lord's property, sanctified to
His use.*"

Since God, according to Palmer, has declared this to be true,
any person who consecrates everything to God can simply claim
sanctification or "holiness." He or she must testify to it publicly,
whether or not he or she receives any inner confirmation from
the Holy Spirit (as Wesley taught) or has an emotional experience. A person simply claims holiness on the basis of faith in
God's promise. Thus Palmer transformed what had been a
lifelong process, the goal of the Christian life for Wesley, into a
momentary experience, the beginning of the "higher life" or
"deeper life" as it came to be termed.

Palmer's teaching, writing (half a dozen books), preaching,
and editing of the *Guide to Holiness* left an indelible impact on
both Methodism and the wider church. Her defense of women's
ministry was only the first of many in the holiness-Pentecostal
tradition which led such churches to ordain women more than
fifty years before more "mainline" denominations began to do so.

Palmer felt that women's ministry was a sign of the dawning of
the kingdom of God on earth. Although she died on November

2, 1874, perhaps she foresaw something of the following century when she noted:

> It is also a significant fact, that to the degree denominations, who have once favored the practice, lose the freshness of their zeal, and as a consequence their primitive simplicity, and, as ancient Israel, yield to a desire to be like surrounding communities, in a corresponding ratio are the labors of females discountenanced.

That is why she also said, "The church in many places is a sort of potter's field, where the gifts of woman, as so many strangers, are buried. How long, O Lord, how long before man shall roll away the stone that we may see a resurrection?" Today, with God's help, the daughters of Sarah and Phoebe are joining to push the stone.

ELIZABETH PRENTISS

Novelist

● While earlier generations had considered the novel a tool of the devil, nineteenth-century women took it up as a means of education and inspiration.

Elizabeth Payson Prentiss (1818–1878) wrote a number of novels for both children and adults, including *Stepping Heavenward,* which was bought by innumerable church libraries.

Elizabeth was the fifth of eight children born to Ann Louisa Shipman of New Haven, Connecticut, and the Rev. Edward Payson, a Harvard graduate and Congregational minister from Rindge, New Hampshire. He served a church in Portland, Maine, for twenty years, where Elizabeth grew up.

Later she admitted that both her theology and piety were deeply influenced by her father. However, when a reader of *Stepping Heavenward* asked if her theology did not come from her father's well-known work, *Thoughts,* she replied somewhat testily that she had not read it in thirty years and "as I am older than my father was when he uttered those thoughts, I have a right to a theology of my own!"

Elizabeth experienced conversion in 1831 and joined the Bleecker Street Presbyterian Church in New York City, where the family had moved following her father's death in 1827. After completing her education, she became a teacher.

On April 16, 1845, she married George Lewis Prentiss, recently ordained pastor of the South Trinitarian Church of New Bedford, Massachusetts—so named to indicate that it was an orthodox Congregational church, in contrast to others which had become Unitarian. During their five years there two children were born: Anna Louise and Edward Payson, who died at age four. In 1851 the family moved to New York City so Mr. Prentiss could pastor the Mercer Street Presbyterian Church. Elizabeth, born in 1852, lived only one month; but Mary, George, and Henry lived to adulthood.

In 1853, in the midst of caring for a house full of toddlers, Prentiss began her literary career with the publication of the first of many children's books: *Little Susy's Six Birthdays,* followed by *Little Susy's Six Teachers,* and *Little Susy's Little Servants.* All of her children's books taught simple truths by example and allegory. In her later books, Prentiss's realistic accounts of children's hijinks and trials set a new trend in juvenile literature.

Her most successful book was *Stepping Heavenward,* first serialized in *The Chicago Advance,* and then published as a book in 1869. There followed at least six London editions, numerous German printings, and editions in Australia, Switzerland, and France.

The novel is the semi-autobiographical journal of one Katherine Mortimer, who marries a Dr. Ernest Elliott and has six children. As Katy says, "Next to being a perfect wife I want to be a perfect mother." She also wants to be a perfect Christian. She is spurred in her spiritual growth by her husband's initial insensitivity to the demands of a busy household, the death of a child, the never-ending drudgery of housewifery, and finally her own terminal seven-year illness. At one point Katy exclaims: "I should like to know if there is any reason on earth why a woman should learn self-forgetfulness that does not apply to a man?"

The purpose of this and her other works is explained in the book's preface. Prentiss writes, "The aim of [my] writings, whether designed for young or old, is to incite to patience, fidelity, hope and all goodness by showing how trust in God and loving obedience to his blessed will will brighten the darkest paths and make a heaven upon earth."

Always in frail health, she believed that suffering "*might* be God's way of preparing his children for very high degrees of service on earth, or happiness in heaven." In this she was encouraged by the reading of such mystics as Archbishop Fenelon and Madame Guyon. Says her husband in her biography, "She came to regard suffering, when sanctified by the Word of God and by prayer, as the King's highway to Christian perfection."

Yet in spite of her suffering and her large family, which she moved each summer to their cottage in Dorset, Vermont, she managed to write at least a book each year—children's books, novels, and poetry.

Her most famous poem is the much-loved hymn, "More Love to Thee, O Christ," probably written in 1856 as a prayer put to verse. Her poetry was such a private expression of her heart that she did not begin sharing it with her husband or friends until 1870. She died August 13, 1878. One verse of her hymn sums up her life:

> Let sorrow do its work,
> Come grief and pain;
> Sweet are thy messengers,
> Sweet their refrain,
> When they can sing with me,
> More love, O Christ, to thee,
> More love to thee,
> More love to thee.

ANTOINETTE BROWN

Minister of the Gospel

● I was reasoned with, pleaded with, and besought even with tears... not to combat a beneficent order tending to promote harmony... in the family and in the commonwealth. Established, ordained masculine headship everywhere was held to be indispensable to morality, and grounded in the inmost fitness of things.

Antoinette Brown (1825–1921) was told she was upsetting the moral order of the universe when she revealed to friends and family that she felt called to be an ordained minister.

Even Lucy Stone, her friend and an avowed advocate of "woman's rights" who thought her "frivolous and feminine" for wearing a flowered hat, considered her dream impossible. When Brown returned to Oberlin College, their alma mater, to study theology, Stone accused her of being there on "dishonorable terms." Said Brown,

I came back here just upon no terms at all. They refused to receive me in the Institution. I came back to study Theology and get knowledge. I do get it; they don't interfere. I am not responsible for their conduct or decisions. . . . I am bound to put myself into the most favorable position for improvement possible while the day for improvement lasts. . . . And what if they or anybody else think I act unwisely, or dishonorably, or foolishly, what can that be to me? I respect their advice, but I do not abide by their decisions.

She attended all of the classes and completed the work, though her name was never listed with the male students nor would the school give her a degree. Despite protests from her fellow students, school authorities would neither allow her to preach in nearby churches nor arrange for her ordination as they did for male students. Brown was on her own.

She had been born on May 20, 1825, the seventh of ten children. Her parents, Joseph and Abby Morse Brown, lived in Henrietta, New York, a village south of Rochester. Though he felt called to the ministry, her father was a farmer and village magistrate. He had been converted during Charles Grandison Finney's famous revival in 1830 in Rochester. He became a deacon at the Congregational church where Antoinette publicly confessed her own religious faith and joined the church at age nine. As a child she led hymns and even preached on occasion.

Valuing education, Antoinette's parents sent her to the Monroe County Academy, where with the exception of Greek, she was allowed to master the same subjects as the men students preparing for Dartmouth. But Antoinette was anxious to follow her older brother William to the country's only coed college, Oberlin, in Ohio, where "our beloved Professor Finney" taught theology.

Warned to steer clear of that "radical" Lucy Stone, Brown sought her out immediately and they became fast friends, and eventually sisters-in-law.

She entered Oberlin in 1845 at age twenty. Her preparation

had been so thorough that she was placed in the same third year course of studies with Lucy, seven years her senior. She completed the college course and began theological studies in 1848. One of her professors told her "he had conscientious scruples in reference to young ladies' delivering orations and preaching sermons," but Dr. Finney let her participate fully in class, and she even led devotions. He also would put the students' names in a hat, draw one out and ask that student to extemporize for as long as possible on the subject at hand. Antoinette's name turned up often and the training gave her skill as an orator and debater.

In March, 1848, she wrote Lucy, "I have been examining the Bible position of woman a good deal this winter reading various commentaries, comparing them with each other and with the Bible and hunting up every passage in the Scriptures that has any bearing on the subject either near or remote." She wrote a paper on the subject and presented it in class. The debate about it was vociferous.

When President Asa Mahan heard about the uproar, he asked to read the paper and had it printed in the next edition of the *Oberlin Quarterly Review*. Antoinette's paper, titled "Exegesis of I Corinthians, xiv, 34, 35; and I Timothy, ii, 11, 12," argued that these verses, which have been used to prohibit women's preaching, were rather intended to silence disruptive chattering and enable women to learn so that they could preach when duly empowered and ordained. It was followed by a rebuttal by her professor, and the next issue carried an article by an alumnus supporting her position.

Brown completed her studies in 1850; the college waited until 1878 to award her an M.A. They gave her an honorary D.D. in 1908.

She was offered a job with the Five Points Mission in New York City. Phoebe Palmer, one of the founders, took her to a meeting the first Sunday, in which they both participated. During the following week, before actually taking up her duties at the mission, Brown attended the first National Woman's Rights

Convention in Worcester, Massachusetts, and spoke in refutation of "the so-called biblical arguments against the public speaking of women." The women of the New York mission were not ready for such radical ideas, and so Antoinette's job plans were revised. She became a lecturer.

On September 15, 1853, Brown finally realized her dream. She became the first woman officially ordained by a recognized denomination in this country. She became minister of the First Congregational Church in Butler and Savannah, New York. The ceremony took place in the local Baptist church because the Congregational church was too small. The sermon was preached by Luther Lee, a Methodist minister and a founder of the Wesleyan Methodist Church. His text was Galatians 3:28, "There is neither Jew nor Greek, there is neither bond nor free, there is neither male nor female: for ye are all one in Christ Jesus."

That fall Brown was an accredited delegate from the South Butler Temperance Society to what was billed as the "World's Temperance Convention" in New York City. She soon learned that the "World" did not include women. When she rose to speak, thanking delegates for voting to seat women delegates,

> There was a great furor, and I stood on the platform for three hours except when someone brought me a chair, and I did not have a chance to open my mouth. So much stamping and pounding with canes that the air was full of dust. . . . Regular hubbub!

She returned two more days with the same results, which moved Horace Greeley to write in the *Tribune:* "First day—Crowding a woman off the platform. Second day—Gagging her. Third day—Voting that she shall stay gagged. Having thus desposed of the main question, we assume the incidentals will be finished this evening."

When asked why she continued in the face of such opposition, Brown noted that "there came rushing over my soul the words of Christ, 'I came not to send peace, but a sword.'" In the midst of the confusion she said, ". . . above me, and within me, and all around me, there was a Spirit stronger than them all."

However, when she returned to her church in South Butler, her spirit became troubled. She refused a mother's request to preach hell-fire and damnation to her dying son. Instead, Brown offered him God's love and saw the child die at peace. The same mother caused further dissension in the parish by objecting when Brown refused to preach on infant damnation and the evils of fornication at the funeral of an illegitimate infant.

Discouraged and shaken in her own faith, Brown was on July 20, 1854, "at her own request" relieved of her duties.

She continued to lecture at woman's rights conventions. The *History of Woman's Suffrage* notes, "Antoinette Brown was called on as usual to meet the Bible argument"; and Brown "made a logical argument on woman's position in the Bible, claiming her complete equality with man, the simultaneous creation of the sexes, and their moral responsibilities as individual and imperative."

Brown returned to New York City to work for a year in the slums and prisons, because, as she said, "I pity the man or woman who does not choose to be identified with the cause of the oppressed." She verbalized her social protest in Horace Greeley's *New York Tribune* and the series of articles became a book, *Shadows of Our Social System* (1856).

In the midst of this changing time in her life, she met and married Samuel Blackwell of Cincinnati—brother of Henry (Lucy Stone's husband) and of Elizabeth and Emily (pioneering physicians). They were married on January 24, 1856. Five of the seven children they bore survived: Florence, Edith, Grace, Agnes, and Ethel.

For the next eighteen years Antoinette rarely appeared on a public platform, but as she says in *The Sexes Throughout Nature*, published in 1875, she maintained a schedule of "three hours of daily habitual brain work, not including daily papers and miscellaneous light reading." The result was a series of books, including several novels and heavier works which sought to understand and resolve the emerging tensions between science and religion.

She never gave up her aspirations to the ministry. In 1878, she announced her availability as a Unitarian minister. When a friend inquired why she had changed churches, she wrote,

> It had long been my one study to reconcile natural and revealed religion, to make the one justify the other; to make them harmonise at points. . . . For a long time this theory worked extremely well. . . . But at length, points arose which would not fit together under the old methods of interpretation.

After Samuel's death in 1901, Antoinette lived with her daughters. In Elizabeth, New Jersey, she founded All Souls' Unitarian Church, which she served until her death. When she was past eighty, she traveled to Alaska and to the Holy Land, bringing back water from the River Jordan to baptize her grandchildren.

Only she of all the original advocates of woman's rights survived to exercise the right to vote on November 2, 1920. Brown died on November 5, 1921.

Despite the pressures from within and without, Antoinette Brown Blackwell responded to God's call to the ministry. In her memoirs she reveals that Charles Finney's first wife, Lydia Andrews,

> having heard that I intended to study theology appealed to me not to do so, at least not to become a public speaker or a minister. When she had brought many stereotyped arguments, her last appeal was, "You will never feel yourself wise enough to go directly against the opinions of all the great men of the past." As that was exactly what her husband had done and was doing, it was necessary for me to reply, "That is exactly what Professor Finney is doing, and we all feel that he is making a great advance of thought."

Later she says, "the second Mrs. Finney," Elizabeth Ford Atkinson, who had a very successful ministry of her own, "was very liberal and said, 'Antoinette, always follow your own convictions.'"

CATHERINE BOOTH

Cofounder of Salvation Army

● "I love my sex. I desire above all earthly things their moral and intellectual elevation. I believe it would be the greatest boon to our race." So said Catherine Booth (1829–90), cofounder of the Salvation Army and a lifelong advocate of women's rights.

She was born on January 17, 1829, in Ashbourne, Derbyshire, England, the only daughter in a family of five children. She learned to read by age three, and by the time she was twelve she had read through the Bible eight times. Though she had little formal schooling, she read voraciously, her subjects including theology and church history.

Her father, John Mumford, was a gifted lay preacher, but his faith faltered and he began to spend more time in coach building (though in later life he did come back to God under the preaching of his daughter.) He remained active in the temperance movement, however, and at age twelve Catherine was writing letters to temperance journals under a *nom de plume.*

At age sixteen she was converted and joined the Wesleyan

Church. One Sunday when she was twenty-two, an itinerate evangelist named William Booth preached in her church. She was impressed with his sermon and a mutual friend relayed the compliment. Soon they were corresponding.

Catherine had very definite ideas about what she wanted in a husband—the same qualities she expected in any deep friendship. First, he must be a true Christian. Second, he should be a man of common sense: "I knew that I could never respect a fool, or one much weaker mentally than myself." Third, husband and wife should have a "oneness of views and tastes, any idea of lordship or ownership being lost in love." If a difference of opinion arose, each should set forth their views and then either one would convince the other or a compromise would evolve. And fourth, her mate must be a total abstainer from liquor by his own convictions and not just to please her.

Sometime after their engagement in May, 1852, William made the mistake of writing her that while he had high regard for woman, he felt she had "a fibre more in her heart and a cell less in her brain." Catherine replied that she would not marry a man who did not consider her and treat her as a complete equal. Thus woman's rights became a major issue in their courtship.

Catherine believed that woman's subjection to man had only been by force and under the curse of the fall. This curse is totally cancelled by Christ's death and resurrection. Even in marriage "the wife may realize as blissful and perfect a oneness with her husband as though it had never been pronounced."

In regard to the church, she cried:

Oh, that the ministers of religion would search the original records of God's Word in order to discover whether the general notions of society are not wrong on this subject, and whether God really intended woman to bury her gifts and talents, as she now does, with reference to the interests of his Church. Oh, that the Church generally would inquire whether narrow prejudice and lordly usurpation has not something to do with the circumscribed sphere of woman's religious labours, and whether much of the non-success of the Gospel is not attributable to the restrictions imposed upon the operations of the Holy Ghost in this as well as other particulars.

Catherine's first published writing was a letter to the editor of the Methodist New Connection magazine in 1854, where she commented on how to care for newborn souls. Her letter ended with a plea to let women use their gifts: "There seems in many societies a growing disinclination among the female members to engage in prayer, speak in love feasts, band meetings, or in any manner bear testimony for their Lord. . . . And this false God-dishonouring timidity is but too fatally pandered to by the church." She noted, in contrast to our own day, that "in the most cold, formal, and worldly churches of the day we find least of female agency."

In 1855 Catherine and William were still discussing these issues by letter. Catherine declared, "I have searched the Word of God through and through, I have tried to deal honestly with every passage on the subject, not forgetting to pray for light to perceive and grace to submit to the truth, however humiliating to my nature, but I solemnly assert that the more I think and read on the subject, the more satisfied I become of the true and scriptural character of my own views."

William finally conceded: "I would not stop a woman preaching on any account. I would not encourage one to begin. You should preach if you felt moved thereto: felt equal to the task. I would not stay you if I had power to do so. Altho', I should not like it." They were married June 16, 1855.

Though Catherine believed strongly in woman's right to speak, she herself was very timid, and frail in body. She was also pregnant three times in the first four and a half years of marriage. But she was always sending William extracts, summaries of articles, and ideas of her own for his sermons. She gave her first lecture in 1857 on the subject of temperance. She enjoyed it so much she wrote her parents: "I only wish I had begun years ago. Had I been fortunate enough to have been brought up amongst the Primitives [Methodists], I believe I should have been preaching now. . . . Indeed, I felt quite at home on the platform, far more so than I do in the kitchen!"

Gradually Catherine was impelled by God into a more public ministry. In December, 1859, she saw a pamphlet by a neighboring minister attacking woman's right to preach. He was upset by the powerful ministry of American evangelist Phoebe Palmer. Encouraged by William, Catherine wrote a stinging rebuttal titled *Female Ministry, or Woman's Right to Preach the Gospel.*

She noted that women in the early church did pray and prophesy publicly and that this was predicted by the prophet Joel as a distinguishing mark of the gospel dispensation. To prove her point she cited various Greek scholars plus biblical examples such as Deborah, Huldah, Miriam, and Anna. She concluded:

> If the Word of God forbids female ministry, we would ask how it happens that so many of the most devoted handmaidens of the Lord have felt themselves constrained by the Holy Ghost to exercise it. Surely there must be some mistake somewhere, for the Word and the Spirit cannot contradict each other. Either the Word does not condemn women preaching, or else those confessedly holy women have been deceived.

Shortly after she finished her pamphlet, her daughter Emma was born. During her confinement, Catherine was deeply convicted by the Spirit that she should consecrate herself to ministry. "I had no vision, but a revelation to my mind." After a struggle, she gave in and vowed to use all her talents for God.

Three months later, having forgotten her promise, she was in a service at their parish in Bethesda. William called for testimonies in the morning service and suddenly the Spirit said to her, "Now if you were to go and testify, you know I would bless it to your own soul as well as to the people." After an inner battle, she finally went forward. She confessed to the congregation that while they thought her a faithful, devoted, proper pastor's wife, she had been unfaithful to the gifts God had given her by not having a more public ministry. She told them of her vow.

William was astounded—but delighted, because he had been urging her for years to address meetings. He immediately asked her to preach that evening. She chose the text, "Be filled with the Spirit."

As always, God's timing was perfect, for William soon took sick with a sore throat and had to be in bed for two weeks. She wrote her parents: "William is, of course, well pleased, and says he felt quite comfortable at home minding the bairns, knowing who was supplying his place." Not long after, he had a complete breakdown due to exhaustion and she took over the entire ministry of his circuit.

Soon Catherine was well versed in all aspects of the ministry. Both yearned to leave the pastorate and become evangelists. But year after year the Methodist connection denied their request. Finally, at the yearly meeting William could take no more. He looked up to Catherine listening in the balcony; she nodded assent, and together they walked out of the building—and out of the denomination. They were on their own with no church and no money—only a vision of what God wanted them to do.

Slowly their mission began to evolve. As one biographer notes, "It was she, and not William Booth, who laid the first stone of the Salvation Army." It was Catherine who, while conducting a mission in 1865 among prostitutes in southeast London, realized that they must forsake the respectable chapels and reach out to the urban masses with the gospel. Before her death in 1890, Catherine had preached to millions.

Though Salvation Army letterheads and news stories today declare, "William Booth, Founder," the title of her biography is more accurate: *Catherine Booth, the Mother of the Salvation Army.*

FRANCES WILLARD

Christian Crusader

● One woman stands among this nation's "statesmen" in our capitol's Hall of Statuary: Frances Elizabeth Caroline Willard. Indeed, she had such an impact on her times that in 1899, a year after her death, Illinois chose her as one of its two representatives.

Most closely identified with the Women's Christian Temperance Union, Willard is sometimes viewed as an eccentric do-gooder, a well-intentioned but unrealistic woman who simplistically thought alcohol the source of all evil. Some undoubtedly confuse her ideas with the ax-wielding fanaticism of Carrie Nation.

Temperance, however, was only one "cause" in Willard's life. Hers was a "do-everything" policy. She devoted her life to work "among the class that I have always loved and that has loved me always—the girls of my native land and my times." From girlhood Willard "revolted against the purely artificial limitations which prevented woman's participation in all the professions."

Her feminism and her temperance stand were rooted in the evangelical revivalism of the mid-nineteenth century, which also spawned the abolition of slavery. She was born on September 28, 1839, in Churchville, New York, fourteen miles from Rochester, the heart of the "Burned-Over District," which was swept by innumerable revivals. In 1841 the family moved to Oberlin, Ohio, the site of the nation's first coeducational college, Oberlin College. Revivalist Charles Finney was professor of theology there and pastor of First Congregational Church. Frances's father and mother both took classes at the college. Even then, three-year-old Frances mimicked the cadence and gestures of the students practicing for their speech classes.

In 1845 the Willard family moved to a farm near Jaynesville, Wisconsin, and switched from Congregationalism to Methodism. When Frances entered Northwestern Female College, the Willards moved to Evanston, Illinois.

Frances experienced conversion in June, 1859, when a case of typhoid fever brought her face to face with death. She described it as a contest between two presences, one "warm, sunny, safe," the other "cold, dismal, dark, with the flutter of a bat." Eventually she responded: "If God lets me get well, I'll try to be a Christian girl." The next winter she affirmed her faith during revival services at Evanston's First Methodist Church. She became a full member on May 5, 1861.

In the winter of 1866, evangelists "Dr. and Mrs. Phoebe Palmer," as she called them, came to Evanston. Under their ministry, Willard experienced the "filling of the Holy Spirit," "holiness," or "Christian perfection." In seeking this experience, she says, "My chief besetments were, as I thought, a speculative mind, a hasty temper, a too ready tongue, and a purpose to be a celebrated person." But the Spirit instead convicted her of her love for fine clothes and jewelry. In surrendering to God, she found "great peace," a "deep welling up of joy" and a sense of the "conscious, emotional presence of Christ."

But these feelings did not last long. Being young and pliable,

Frances bowed to the advice of her male superiors at the Genesee Wesleyan Seminary in Lima, New York, where she went to teach. They advised her to keep quiet about her experience, since some people regarded it as controversial. She said she soon found she had little to speak about.

Later in life Willard freely admitted that her first desire had been to share her brother's call to the ministry:

> The deepest thought and desire of my life would have been met, if my dear old Mother Church had permitted me to be a minister. The wandering life of an evangelist or a reformer comes nearest to, but cannot fill, the ideal which I early cherished, but did not expect ever publicly to confess.
>
> I was too timid to go without a call; and so it came about that while my unconstrained preference would long ago have led me to the pastorate, I have failed of it.

Eventually she wrote *Woman in the Pulpit* (1888), arguing women's right to be ordained and urging them to seek seminary training.

Throughout her life, Willard worked hard for the Methodist church. In 1865–66 she served as corresponding secretary for the American Methodist Ladies Centenary Association. She helped to raise thirty thousand dollars to build Garrett Seminary's Heck Hall—named for Barbara Heck, whom some call the founder of the Methodist church in America. At the building's dedication, however, not one woman graced the platform. Willard wrote a speech, but a man read it. Such were the customs of the day.

Willard also tried her hand at revivalism. In 1877 D. L. Moody asked her to hold "ladies' meetings" every afternoon as part of his attempt to revive Boston. Although she enjoyed preparing her Bible studies and leading the services, she felt constricted by Moody's limitations on her ministry, and so they parted ways.

Her affair with the church was sometimes a lovers' quarrel. In 1880 Willard stopped by the Methodist church's General Conference simply to bring greetings from the W.C.T.U., a common custom among organizations. She was aghast when a motion to allow her ten minutes to speak provoked two hours of acrimonious debate. Although her request finally received a favorable vote, she withdrew, leaving only a note to be read by a man. In her W.C.T.U. presidential address that year, she did indulge in a parting thrust by quoting Finney: "The church that silences the women is shorn of half its power."

In 1888 Willard and four other women were duly elected delegates to the General Conference. After another lengthy and vicious debate, the women were denied seats. Willard was so angry and disappointed that in her presidential address that year she threatened to withdraw from the church and to found one of her own:

> The time will come, however, and not many years from now, when if representation is still denied us, it will be our solemn duty to raise once more the cry, "here I stand, I can do no other," and step out into the larger liberty of a religious movement, where majorities and not minorities determine the fitness of women as delegates, and where the laying on of hands in consecration, as was undoubtedly done in the early church, shall be decreed on a basis of "gifts, graces and usefulness," irrespective of sex.

Denied access to the ministry, Frances Willard's first commitment was to women's education. After about four years of formal education, she graduated in 1859 from Northwestern Female College. After teaching for several years, she became president of Evanston College for Ladies. But before she could preside over the college, she had to raise money to build it. She engineered a cornerstone-laying and pledge-solicitation on July 4, 1871, and the school opened that fall. Some credit her as the first woman college president ever to bestow degrees that next spring, but it was the school's first and last graduation. The 1871 Chicago fire had destroyed the resources of those who had signed pledges, and the college merged with Northwestern University.

Willard was made dean of women for the university, but unfortunately the president, a rejected suitor, so undermined her authority and humiliated her that within a year she resigned.

Shortly thereafter the women of Ohio began the Temperance Crusade. Willard, a delegate from the Evanston society to the first national convention in 1874, became corresponding secretary. Her goals were broader than controlling the liquor traffic; they were essentially to gain political power for women. She once commented, "I always thought that next to a wish I had to be a saint some day, I would really like to be a politician." And so she was.

She recalled the day in 1851 when news reached Wisconsin that Maine had passed a law prohibiting liquor sales. That night her father mused, "I wonder if poor, rum-cursed Wisconsin will ever get a law like that?" Her mother rocked a time in silence and then replied, "Yes, Josiah, there'll be such a law all over the land some day, when women vote." Her father, "a great conservative," was "tremendously astonished" to hear such talk from his wife. Sarcastically he queried, "And pray how will you arrange it so that women shall vote?" The rocker moved more swiftly and Mary Willard's eyes focused on the fire: "Well, I say to you, as the apostle Paul said to his jailor, 'You have put us into prison, we being Romans, and you must come and take us out.'"

Initially Frances Willard held back from the woman's rights movement which had been organized at Seneca Falls in 1848. As one biographer says, in the 1870s, "suffrage was too advanced and radical a thing, connected in those days with too much ridicule and scorn, a thing unwomanly and unscriptural, and to touch it was contamination."

Yet, one Sunday morning in May, 1876, as Willard was engaged in Bible study and prayer before a speech she was to give in Columbus, Ohio,

There was borne in upon my mind, as I believe, from loftier regions, the declaration, "You are to speak for woman's ballot as a weapon of protection to her home and tempted loved ones from the tyranny of drink," and then for the first and only time in my life, there flashed through my brain, a complete line of argument and illustration. . . .

When she arrived at the W.C.T.U.'s annual convention that October, she felt that "woe is me if I declare not this gospel." So she spoke, beginning with an anecdote about a black man who, in the act of saving the lives of three white comrades in the Civil War, shouted: "Somebody's got to be killed, and it might as well be me." Her friends wept, she said, "at the thought of ostracism which, from that day to this, has been its sequel."

At the end of Willard's speech, the chairwoman dissociated the W.C.T.U. with the sentiments she had expressed, declaring, "We do not propose to trail our skirts through the mire of politics." Willard, however, said she "felt far more strongly the undergirdings of the Spirit" who evidently was moving. At that meeting Hannah Whitall Smith, already famous for *The Christian's Secret of a Happy Life,* found an older woman sobbing bitterly. Trying to comfort her, Smith asked the cause of her tears. She replied: "Frances Willard has just convinced me that I ought to want to vote, and I *don't want to!*" Another woman, possibly Smith herself, who had remained aloof from the suffragists because of doubts of their orthodoxy, now felt dutybound to join the cause. So, she said,

> I asked God to gather up my prejudices as a bundle and lay them aside. They remained tangible and tough, but I laid them aside. . . . It came after nights of waking and weeping, for I felt the dear Lord was preparing me for something, and He did not want me to be burdened with that bundle.

Reaction was so strong that Willard dropped out of temperance work for about a year. But then as president she led the Illinois Union in a "home protection campaign" to secure the right of women to vote on temperance issues. Within three months the women collected 180,000 signatures which they presented to the state legislature on a white muslin roll a quarter of a mile long. Songs, prayers, and parades in the capital were unavailing. Members became convinced that "while prohibition is the nail, woman's ballot is the hammer that must drive it home."

Backed by the women of Illinois, Willard went to the national convention in 1879 and, as leader of a "liberal" wing, unseated the old guard. She held complete control of the organization for the next sixteen years. She traveled to make the membership nationwide; she reorganized its structure to make it more effective; she got a "Franchise Department" and endorsement of an equal suffrage plank. Within the W.C.T.U. she trained the leadership which eventually led the women of America to secure the vote with the Nineteenth Amendment in 1920. Willard, who died in 1898, did not live to see its passage.

Frances Willard succeeded in selling women on their need for suffrage by making it a matter of selfless service rather than selfish "rights." She made it a matter of women's Christian duty. "Not rights, but duties: not her need alone, but that of her children and her country; not the 'woman,' but the 'human' question is stirring women's hearts and breaking down their prejudices to-day," she declared.

Her goal was to make "the whole world homelike" because "what the world most needs is mothering." The key was organization. "We all know that organization is the one great thought of nature," said Willard. "It is the difference between chaos and order; it is the incessant occupation of God. But, next to God, the greatest organizer is the mother. . . . Hence, woman by her organism, is the greatest organizer ever organized by our beneficent Creator."

And Frances Willard—organizer, politician, and Christian woman—was one of the Creator's finest organisms.

AMANDA SMITH

Touring Evangelist

● Many women in the church have been and are gifted evangelists: Phoebe Palmer and Aimee Semple McPherson, Catherine Booth and Kathryn Kuhlman.

Amanda Smith (1837–1915) was an unlikely candidate for this list of Christ's evangels. Born on January 23, 1837, in Long Green, Maryland, she was the oldest daughter of slaves. Her father, Samuel Berry, was offered a chance by the mistress of the farm to buy his freedom when his master died. He earned extra money by making and selling brooms and husk mats, and by working nights on other farms after he had spent the day in his mistress's fields.

Amanda's mother, Miriam Matthews, possessed a vital Christian faith. She prayed especially for the conversion of their master's daughter. Eventually the daughter was converted at a Methodist camp meeting, but soon afterward the girl contracted typhoid. On her deathbed she made her parents promise to let Sam buy the freedom of Miriam and their five children.

The Berry family then moved to Pennsylvania, where their home became a stop on the underground railroad. Amanda learned at an early age what it means to trust God's providence and protection.

She had very little formal schooling. In *An Autobiography: The Story of the Lord's Dealings with Mrs. Amanda Smith, the Colored Evangelist,* she says she went to school for only six weeks in the summers when she was eight and thirteen. She and her brother walked five and a half miles to attend a school, but they got the teacher's attention only after "the requirements of the more favored [i.e., white] pupils had been met." Both of her parents could read so Amanda would cut large letters out of newspapers and have her parents arrange them into words.

When Amanda was thirteen, her mother died and she began to work for a widow with five children in Stroudsburg, Pennsylvania. At the Methodist Episcopal church there a revival broke out. Amanda describes herself as "a poor colored servant girl sitting away back by the door" when a young white woman came and entreated her with tears to accept Christ. "I was the only colored girl there, but I went. She knelt beside me with her arms around me and prayed for me." She went home that night resolved to "be the Lord's and live for Him."

She joined the church and became a member of a class meeting, but eventually she had to give that up because no matter where she sat, the class leader always "led" all the white people first, which made her late for work.

Famous for her Maryland biscuits and fried chicken, she worked hard for various families. At seventeen she married Calvin M. Devine. She says, "He believed in religion for his mother's sake . . . He could talk on the subject of religion very sensibly at times; but when strong drink would get the better of him . . . then he was very profane and unreasonable." They had two children but only their daughter Mazie survived to adulthood. Eventually Calvin enlisted in the Union Army and went South to war, never to return.

Her second husband, James Smith of Philadelphia, was also a disappointment. An ordained deacon in the African Methodist Episcopal Church, he told her he was studying to be licensed as an evangelist. Since she had long felt a similar calling, she thought they could work as a team. So she married him. But when she went to Conference to hear the appointments read out, his name was not among them. He confessed that he had only told her that ambition in order to win her. In fact he became rather indifferent to the faith.

Their marriage produced three children, all of whom died young. She admits, "My mother heart was sad, but nevertheless the Lord stood by me." She and James were often separated because they could not find work in the same areas of New York City where they were then living. Sometimes James' salary was insufficient to support them, so Amanda washed and ironed for people. He died in November, 1869.

In the midst of difficulty, Amanda's spiritual life continued to grow. In 1856 she experienced a revival of her childhood conversion. But "not having proper teaching, like Israel of old, I wandered in the wilderness of doubts and fears, ups and downs, for twelve years." God was disciplining her for service: "He began by degrees to let me down. The Devil turned his hose on me, for it was as though a man was washing a sidewalk or a carriage. He seemed to come to me in various ways, in such power, that I settled down in God."

One Sunday in September, 1868, she decided to go hear Presbyterian evangelist John S. Inskip preach at the Green Street Methodist Church in New York. His message concerning holiness spoke to her heart: "As quick as the spark from smitten steel, I felt the touch of God from the crown of my head to the soles of my feet . . . It seemed to press me gently on the top of my head, and I felt something part and roll down and cover me like a great cloak! It was done in a moment, and O what a mighty peace and power took possession of me!"

Yet she was afraid to go to the altar in the mostly white

church. "Somehow I always had a fear of white people—that is, I was not afraid of them in the sense of doing me harm, or anything of that kind—but a kind of fear because they were white, and were there, and I was black and was here!" But as she walked down the street that day, the Spirit reminded her of Gal. 3:28, her fear drained away and the Son set her free.

Later when women at Ocean Grove, New Jersey, asked her if she would rather be white, she could answer, "I would rather be black and fully saved than be white and not saved; I was bad enough black as I am, and I would have been ten times worse if I had been white." During her public ministry she often found that when people truly got sanctified, God took their prejudice away, but she also admits, "Some people don't get enough of the blessing to take prejudice out of them, even after they are sanctified."

Her race was not the only source of prejudice: "There were then but few of our ministers that were favorable to women's preaching or taking part, I mean in a public way; but, thank God, there always were a few men that dared to stand by a woman's liberty in this way, if God called her."

And God made that call very plain to Amanda. First God gave her a beautiful singing voice. Second, though she was uneducated, she was very articulate in the pulpit. Third, God gave her a vision of the letters GO and a voice said, "Go, preach." Sometimes she hesitated and asked for a sign. God paid her rent in advance and gave her new shoes. Satan questioned her, "When Jesus sent out his disciples he sent them out two and two, and now you are going out alone; they will say you are going to look for a husband." She knew that was not true, but she did long for a woman companion. God finally said, "Go and I will be with you."

She began to travel about the U.S.—to the first black denominational meeting held below the Mason-Dixon line in Knoxville; to Austin, Tex., where she had to sit all night in the railway station because she was black and alone and did not know where to go; to Washington, D.C., where she was invited to speak but had to walk around for two days before she could find a restaurant to serve her. She wore a plain poke bonnet and Quaker dress of brown or black. Her few belongings were in a carpetbag.

Then an invitation came to preach in England. She did not even pray about the matter, thinking it too lofty a request for a poor black woman to make. But God said, "You are afraid to trust the Lord and go to England; you are afraid of the ocean." She admitted it was true and in that moment God showed her a movie of her life, how he had led and provided for her. She felt ashamed and cried, "Lord, forgive me . . . give me another chance, and I will go to England."

God even gave her first-class passage on the ship and an opportunity to hold services for the passengers. She arrived in July, 1878, thinking she would stay three months; it was twelve years before she returned home. After visiting Keswick, she held evangelistic services throughout England and Scotland.

Then she felt led to go to India and Burma, where she stayed for two years, preaching holiness unto the Lord. The foreword to her autobiography is a glowing tribute by J. M. Thoburn, Methodist bishop of India.

Returning to England, she thought she would come home, but God sent her to Africa for the next eight years, mostly into Liberia and Sierra Leone. Until then people had generously supported her work, but suddenly all financial contributions ceased. She wondered why, but God said, "You are not trusting in Me; you are trusting in America." So she asked forgiveness and found that her needs were all met. She even adopted two African children and sent them to England to be educated.

Finally returning to America in 1890, she felt unable to continue touring as an evangelist. She thought her work was finished. But after a rest, she settled down in a suburb of Chicago where she spent her remaining years heading an orphanage for black children. She died February 24, 1915.

Her autobiography ends with the prayer "that many of my own

people will be led to a more full consecration, and that the Spirit of the Lord may come upon some of the younger women who have talent, and who had better opportunities than I have ever had and so must do better work for the Master."

RAMABAI

God's Woman in India

● "O Father of the world, hast Thou not created us? Or has, perchance, some other god made us? Dost Thou care only for men? Hast Thou no thought for us women?"

This heart-cry of a young Hindu widow inspired Ramabai in her efforts to rescue and educate her sisters.

Ramabai (1858–1922) knew well the oppression of women in India. Her father, Anant, was learned in the Sanskrit scriptures. He studied with a teacher in Poona, who taught the local ruler—and the ruler's wife, a thing unheard of in Hindu culture. Anant vowed to educate his wife, Lakshmibai. She was nine and he was forty-four.

Opposition from his relatives and the townspeople was so strong that Anant finally moved his family to the forest of Gungamal, in the Western Ghaut mountains. He became a guru for disciples and pilgrims. His wife, formerly a timid child, blossomed into an able scholar and administrator of their *ashram* (religious retreat). She also gave birth to six children, three of whom survived.

Ramabai was the youngest, born on April 23, 1858, and named for the goddess Rama, whose name means "brightness" or "light." But before Ramabai was six months old, family fortunes declined and she began "pilgrimage" in a woven basket on the head of a servant. Despite the family's wandering life, Lakshmibai tutored her daughter in Sanskrit, the sacred language. By age twelve she had learned 18,000 verses of the Puranas (the poetic scriptures of the common people)—plus the vernacular languages of Marathi, Kanarese, Kindustani, and Bengali, picked up in the course of their travels. The family made its living by reciting the Puranas, which not only gave them religious merit but was also considered meritorious to those listening. Hearers would give them a small coin or handful of rice.

As they moved from shrine to shrine, they bathed in the sacred waters of rivers, lakes, tanks, hoping to free themselves from sin. Once they camped for an entire year at Kwarka on the Arabian Sea because it was thought to contain all the sacred waters together. It was believed that those who bathed in the sea every day for a year obtained extraordinary merit. That year, Ramabai's thirteenth, contained a very sacred day marked by the conjunction of certain planets—an event which happens only every sixty years. According to local priests, all who bathed in the sea and gave alms on that day would be sinless and rewarded by a vision of Krishna's sacred city. Even then, Ramabai later said, she realized that "the sins remained where they were, as before" and that what she witnessed that day was no more than the setting sun painting the clouds golden over the sea.

When Ramabai was sixteen, a devastating famine began which seared the Madras Presidency for three years. Within six weeks both of her parents and her sister died. Only she and her brother were left. They continued their life of pilgrimage, arriving in Calcutta in 1878, where they gave lectures and won the hearts of Bengali Brahmans. Ramabai's learning so impressed them that after examination by a group of scholars she was given the title *Saraswati*, the "divine embodiment of language, literary expression and learning." From then on she was referred to as "Pandita Ramabai," the learned Ramabai.

But tragedy continued to haunt her. Weakened by years of privation, Ramabai's brother died in 1880. Alone in the world, she decided to marry. By Hindu custom her father, as a good Brahman, should have arranged her marriage when she was between the ages of 5 and 11, but he allowed her to wait until she was grown. He also decided to allow her to marry the man of her choice. She chose Bepin Bihari Medhavi, a lawyer, a graduate of Calcutta University, and a Sudra—one of a much lower caste than her own. Because both had lost faith in traditional Hinduism, they were married in a civil ceremony.

After only nineteen months of marriage, Ramabai's husband died of cholera on February 4, 1882. Her only consolation was their child, her daughter Manoramabai, "heart's joy."

Ramabai had begun to have grave doubts about Hinduism. Her parents had been devout, yet they had died of starvation. In Calcutta, she had met Hindus who were theistic—that is, they believed in God but they repudiated superstition and the multiplicity of idols. One such Hindu urged her to study the sacred Vedas and the Upanishads, which even her father had not dared teach her or her mother.

As she read, she says in *A Testimony*, "My eyes were being gradually opened; I was waking up to my own hopeless condition as a woman." She realized that "women of high caste and low caste as a class were bad, very bad, worse than demons, as holy as untruth, and that they could not get *Moksha* [liberation] as men [could]." Their only hope of surcease from the endless round of reincarnation, was "worship of their husbands." According to the Hindu sacred law, the Code of Manu, "Though destitute of virtue, or seeking pleasure elsewhere, or devoid of good qualities, yet as a husband he must be constantly worshipped as a god by a faithful wife . . . if a wife obeys her husband, she will for that reason alone be exalted in heaven."

A good wife must bear sons: "There is no place for a man [in heaven] who is destitute of male offspring." Widowhood was regarded "as the punishment for a horrible crime or crimes committed by the woman in her former existence upon earth." A Hindu proverb declared that "Woman is a great whirlpool of suspicion, a dwelling-place of vices, full of deceits, a hindrance in the way of heaven, the gate of hell." A woman suspected of being disobedient in some way to her husband was often later accused of being the cause of his death. It was popular belief that a husband would die if his wife learned to read or write.

In Calcutta Ramabai had been given a Sanskrit Bible, but she found it difficult to understand. In her husband's library she found a more interesting pamphlet—the Gospel of Luke in Bengali. At that time she was also visited by a Baptist missionary who began to explain the Bible to her. Her husband, learning of her interest, forbade the missionary to visit again. "I had lost all faith in my former religion," she said, "and my heart was hungering after something better."

After her husband's death, Ramabai formed a woman's society, *Arya Mahila Somaj,* to work for the deliverance of women from the evils of child-marriage, ignorance, and religious oppression. And she began to study the New Testament with Church of England missionaries. She learned English, and desired further study in England.

In 1883 she sailed for England, where she and her daughter spent a year with the sisters of the Community of St. Mary the Virgin at Wantage. The sisters taught her English, the Christian faith, and secular subjects. They also impressed her with their mission work in London among prostitutes: "Here for the first time in my life, I came to know that something could be done to reclaim the so-called fallen women." When she asked what motivated the sisters' compassion, they read her John 4, the story of Jesus' encounter with the woman of Samaria. Suddenly, Ramabai realized that "Christ was truly the Divine Saviour He claimed to be, and no one but He could transform and uplift the down-trodden womanhood of India and of every land." On September 29, 1883, Ramabai and Manoramabai were baptized into the Christian faith.

After further education in England and the United States, and publication of *The High Caste Hindu Woman* (1887), she returned to India in 1888 supported by the Ramabai Society, which had pledged to support her educational work with five thousand dollars per year for ten years. In Poona she founded a school for Brahman child-widows, the *Sarada Sadan,* "Home of Wisdom," where girls were taught basic and useful subjects. Both the Bible and the Hindu scriptures were in the library, and students practiced their Hindu customs without disturbance. Ramabai also practiced her Christian faith. She refused to close the door of her room while she and her daughter had family devotions. Soon students gathered to listen and finally in November, 1895, in spite of Ramabai's objections, twelve girls of Sarada Sadan confessed faith in Christ by baptism.

As Ramabai knew it would, a storm of protest broke out. Many families withdrew their daughters, but Ramabai's faith was unshaken and her principles unchanged. The school weathered the storm. However, when she reorganized the school in 1898, she made it a Christian institution.

In 1896 a major famine spread through the central provinces of India. Stirred by memories of her family's plight, Ramabai went out to gather the girls widowed by the famine. Soon she had hundreds under her care. With the threat of plague, she moved them to some farm land she had acquired outside Poona, at Kedgoan. Inspired by the "faith-work" of George Müller, the German evangelist in Bristol, England, she took in hundreds of child-widows—and the food supply never failed nor did the deep wells go dry. In 1900 another severe famine struck the Gujarat province. Though she already had 1,900 women at the Mukti

Mission in Kedgoan, she took in 1,350 Gujarati girls. In order to be self-supporting, the girls worked in the weaving sheds, blacksmith shop, book bindery, tannery, cobbler shop, carpentry shop, and tin shop.

God did not fail them physically or spiritually. Ramabai was able to house, feed, clothe, and educate her "household," and God sent revival as well. In December, 1901, twelve hundred girls professed faith. Ramabai felt they needed to deepen their faith, and so in 1905 she formed a special prayer circle of seventy to pray for a special outpouring of the Holy Spirit. There followed a great revival which paralleled in many ways the beginnings of Pentecostalism being experienced in America.

In the midst of supervising a burgeoning mission complex, Ramabai devoted her last fifteen years to translating the entire Bible into Marathi, using words even poorly educated women could read and understand. To do this, Ramabai had to master Greek and Hebrew. In her last months she corrected the final proofs and the women in her household rushed to begin the printing. When Ramabai fell ill, she asked God for ten more days to complete the proofreading. She got exactly that and died in her sleep on April 5, 1922. The work at Mukti Mission, "the home of salvation," continues.

LUCY PEABODY

Missionary Organizer

● The missionary enterprise abroad has always been supported by the efforts of innumerable women in this country—the women who paid their dues to the "Cent Societies," the women who sold eggs, butter, and even their extra dresses and petticoats to earn fifty cents or a dollar for the missionaries.

Through the years their efforts were encouraged and coordinated by energetic workers such as Lucy Peabody (1861–1949) and Helen Barrett Montgomery (1861–1934).

Lucy Whitehead McGill, born in Belmont, Kansas, was reared in Rochester, New York. After graduating from high school, she taught in a school for deaf children. Soon she met Norman Waterbury, a seminarian, who asked her if she would go to the mission field with him. In 1881, a month after their marriage, they sailed for Madras, India, as members of the American Baptist Missionary Union.

Soon Norman was busy translating the New Testament into Telegu, the Dravidian language spoken in the area. Though Lucy gave birth to two children within the next two years, she taught Indian women and children, and was delighted with her work. In 1886, however, Norman died, and shortly thereafter Lucy was forced to return to Rochester, a widow with two small children.

To support her family, Lucy began teaching deaf children again. One night she was asked to talk about foreign missions at a meeting in Penfield, New York. Also at that meeting was Helen Barrett Montgomery, who had come to talk about home missions. The two were to become a team.

Montgomery was born to A. Judson and Emily Barrett July 31, 1861, in Kingsville, Ohio, where her father was a school principal. When Helen was seven the family moved to Lowville, New York. Eventually her father graduated from Rochester Theological Seminary and became pastor of the Lake Avenue Baptist Church in Rochester. Helen graduated from Wellesley, and taught for several years. When her father died in 1889, she was licensed to preach and served his church as its pastor until a successor was named.

On September 6, 1887, Helen married William A. Montgomery, a manufacturer seven years her senior. They adopted a daughter, Edith, in 1890. Founder and twenty-year president of the Rochester Women's Educational and Industrial Union, Helen was elected to the school board, which she served for ten years. She also chaired a committee which raised a hundred thousand dollars to help Rochester University become coed.

In April, 1889, Lucy Waterbury moved her family to Boston to work for the Women's Baptist Foreign Missionary Society. Soon she was head of the organization. In 1900 she formed a Central Committee for the United Study of Foreign Missions, whose purpose was to educate women in all churches about missions so that they could give more intelligently. She led the Central Committee for 28 years. Helen Montgomery organized a summer school program to train study leaders, and also wrote several of the annual study guides.

Henry Wayland Peabody was an importer-exporter from Boston, and a widower. He was also president of the Board of Managers of the Baptist Missionary Union, where he met Lucy Waterbury. He asked her to marry him, and, although he was twenty years older than she, she agreed. Sadly, he died two years later, and Lucy gave her fortune and all her energies again to missionary work.

Part of that energy went into a mission celebration. Lucy realized that 1911 would be the fifty-year anniversary of the Women's Union Missionary Society of America for Heathen Lands, founded by Sarah Doremus. In just fifty years, women had raised more than forty-one million dollars for that organization. To celebrate, Lucy asked Helen Montgomery to write a book about single women missionaries. The result was *Western Women in Eastern Lands*, which sold 50,000 copies in its first six weeks.

Lucy also organized rallies across the country. Within a two-month period she, Helen, and about a dozen missionary doctors and teachers each gave about two hundred speeches in seventy major cities and many smaller towns. They arrived home exhausted, but delighted that they had raised $1,030,000, mostly to give to Christian women's colleges in Asia.

In 1913 Peabody proposed that she and Montgomery take their daughters on a round-the-world trip to visit the missions they had done so much to support. Montgomery researched and wrote another study book: *From Campus to World Citizenship*. Both attended a meeting of the Commission on Education which was convening to follow up the historic 1910 World Missionary Conference in Edinburgh. And Lucy attended another international meeting in Holland that fall. Mr. Montgomery commented, "When I married Helen Barrett I realized that she had ability and training to do what I could never do. I resolved, therefore, never to interfere with any call that might come to her. If Helen cares to go, I will help her in every possible way." The four women visited Europe, Egypt, India, China, and Japan.

Inspired by what they had seen, Lucy and Helen in 1920

helped to form a Joint Committee for Women's Union Christian Colleges in Foreign Fields. Lucy was asked to raise one million dollars as a Christmas gift. She raised $767,000.

The committee then felt they could raise another three million dollars. Lucy talked John D. Rockefeller, Jr., into pledging one million dollars if she could match it two to one by January 1, 1923. She threw all her energies into the project. When the deadline came, she had collected $2,942,555!

The money went to seven schools. One was the Isabella Thoburn College in Lucknow, India, founded by the first missionary commissioned by the Women's Foreign Missionary Society of the Methodist Episcopal Church. Isabella went to India in 1869 with Dr. Clara A. Swain, the first woman medical missionary.

A second college was Dr. Ida Scudder's Union Missionary Medical School for Women in Vellore, India.

Other colleges were the Women's Christian College in Madras, where Lucy had worked and her daughter Norma had been born; the women's College of Yenching University in Peking; Ginling College in Nanking; the North China Union Medical College for Women in Peking (which later became part of Shantung Christian University), and the Women's Christian College of Tokyo.

At that time American Christians were being divided by controversies over the "fundamentals" and the "social gospel," but Peabody declared:

Women were unconcerned about whether preaching should be the only object of missions. They did not bother themselves with sophisticated arguments about the social gospel vs. preaching as the only proper form of evangelism. They simply responded to what were obvious needs and that response was their witness and their evangelism.

Montgomery was elected the first president of the combined Woman's American Baptist Foreign Mission Society in 1914, a post which she held for ten years. Peabody was foreign vice president. For that group Helen wrote *Following the Sunrise: A Century of Baptist Missions 1813–1913.*

In 1921–22 Montgomery became the first woman ever to head a major denomination when she was elected president of the American or Northern Baptist Convention. She was also one of the few people to singlehandedly translate the New Testament into English. Since her father was a professor of Latin and Greek, she had gained her language skills early. She completed the translation in 1924. Known as the *Centenary Translation,* or *The New Testament in Modern English,* it is still available from Judson Press.

Through her organizational work and fund raising, together with Helen Barrett Montgomery, Lucy Peabody helped spread the gospel around the world. Her efforts, and the efforts of women like her, not only enabled American missionaries to go overseas, but also helped women in other countries to share the Good News with their people through preaching, teaching, medical aid, and social work.

FOR FURTHER READING

● Resources for exploring the role of women in the life of the church are becoming more numerous. Below are listed some of these sources, old and new, general and specific.

General

Bowie, Walter R. *Women of Light*. New York: Harper & Row, 1963.

Culver, Elsie Thomas. *Women in the World of Religion*. Garden City, N.Y.: Doubleday, 1967.

Deen, Edith. *Great Women of the Christian Faith*. New York: Harper & Brothers, 1959.

Hale, Sarah Josepha. *Woman's Record*. New York: Harper & Brothers, 1853.

Hanaford, Phoebe A. *Daughters of America*. Augusta, Me.: True and Company, 1882.

Mainiero, Lina, ed. *American Women Writers: From Colonial Times to the Present*. New York: Frederick Ungar, 1979.

Notable American Women. Cambridge, Mass.: Belknap Press, 1971.

Marcella and Paula

Palladius. *The Lausiac History*. Translated and edited by W. K. Lowther Clarke. London: Society for Promoting Christian Knowledge, 1918.

Pulcheria

Teetgen, Ada. *The Life and Times of the Empress Pulcheria.* London: Swan Sonnenschein & Company, Ltd., 1907.

Hilda, Leoba, Hroswitha

Bede. *A History of the English Church and People.* London: Penguin Books, Ltd., 1968.

Boniface. *The Letters of Saint Boniface.* Translated by Ephraim Emerton. New York: Farrar, Straus and Giroux, 1973.

Deanesly, Margaret. *The Pre-Conquest Church in England.* London: Adam and Charles Black, 1961.

Eckenstein, Lina. *Woman Under Monasticism: Chapters on Saint-Lore and Convent Life Between* A.D. *500 and* A.D. *1500.* Cambridge: At the University Press, 1896.

Haight, Anne Lyon, ed. *Hroswitha of Gandersheim.* Richmond: University of Virginia, 1978.

Leibell, Helen Dominica. *Anglo-Saxon Education of Women: From Hilda to Hildegarde.* New York: Burt Franklin, 1922.

Levison, Wilhelm. *England and the Continent in the Eighth Century.* Oxford: The Clarendon Press, 1946.

Montalembert, Charles Forbes, and Rene de Tryon, Counte de. *The Monks of the West.* 6 vols. London: John C. Nimmo, 1896.

Morris, Joan. *The Lady Was a Bishop.* New York: Macmillan, 1973.

Rudolf, Monk of Fulda. *The Life of St. Leoba,* in Talbot, C. H. *The Anglo-Saxon Missionaries in Germany.* London: Sheed & Ward, 1954.

Stenton, Doris May. *The English Woman in History.* London: George Allen & Unwin, Ltd., 1957.

Catherine of Siena, Julian of Norwich

Catherine of Siena. *The Dialogue of Saint Catherine of Siena.* Translated by Algar Thorold. Rockford, Ill.: Tan Books and Publishers, 1974.

Giordani, Igino. *Catherine of Siena: Fire and Blood.* Milwaukee: The Bruce Publishing Company, 1959.

Julian of Norwich. *Revelations of Divine Love.* Edited by Clifton Wolters. Baltimore: Penguin Books, 1966.

_____. *A Shewing of God's Love.* Edited by Anna Maria Reynolds. London: Sheed & Ward, 1958.

_____. *Showings.* Edited by Edmund Colledge and James Walsh. New York: Paulist Press, 1978.

Knowles, David. *The English Mystical Tradition.* New York: Harper & Row, 1965.

Power, Eileen. *Medieval Women*. Cambridge: Cambridge University Press, 1975.

Stuard, Susan Mosher, editor. *Women in Medieval Society*. Philadelphia: University of Pennsylvania Press, 1976.

Underhill, Evelyn. *Mysticism*. New York: E. P. Dutton, 1961.

Marguerite of Navarre, Jeanne d'Albret

Bainton, Roland. *Women of the Reformation*. 3 vols. Minneapolis: Augsburg, 1977.

Quaker Women

Best, Mary Agnes. *Rebel Saints*. New York: Harcourt, Brace and Company, 1925.

Braithwaite, William C. *The Beginnings of Quakerism*. Revised second edition by Henry J. Cadbury. Cambridge: At the University Press, 1961.

Luder, Hope Elizabeth. *Women and Quakerism*. Lebanon, Pa.: Sowers Printing Company, Pendle Hill Pamphlet, 1974.

Noble, Vernon. *The Man in Leather Breeches: The Life and Times of George Fox*. New York: Philosophical Library, 1953.

Barbara Heck

Coles, George. *Heroines of Methodism*. New York: Carlton & Porter, [1857].

[Disoway, Gabriel Poillan.] *Our Excellent Women of the Methodist Church in England and America*. New York: J. C. Buttre, 1861.

Keeling, Annie E. *Eminent Methodist Women*. London: Charles H. Kelly, 1889.

Magalis, Elaine. *Conduct Becoming to a Woman: Methodist Women in America*. Cincinnati: Service Center, 1973.

Norwood, Frederick. *The Story of American Methodism*. Nashville: Abingdon Press, 1974.

Stevens, Abel. *The Women of Methodism*. New York: Carlton & Porter, 1866.

Withrow, W. H. *Barbara Heck*. London: Robert Culley, [c. 1894].

Sally Parsons, Clarissa Danforth

Baxter, Norman Allen. *History of the Freewill Baptists*. Rochester, N.Y.: American Baptist Historical Society, [1957].

Stewart, I. D. *The History of the Freewill Baptists*. Freewill Baptist Printing Establishment, 1862.

Isabella Graham, Joanna Bethune

Bethune, George. *Memoirs of Mrs. Joanna Bethune.* New York: Harper & Brothers, 1863.

[Bethune, Joanna.] *The Power of Faith, Exemplified in the Life and Writings of the late Mrs. Isabella Graham.* New York: American Tract Society, 1843.

Foster, Charles I. *An Errand of Mercy: The Evangelical United Front, 1790–1837.* Chapel Hill: The University of North Carolina Press, 1960.

Graham, Isabella. *The Unpublished Letters and Correspondence from the Years 1767 to 1814.* New York: J. S. Taylor, 1838.

Lynn, Robert, and Wright, Elliott. *The Big Little School: Sunday Child of American Protestantism.* New York: Harper & Row, 1971.

Mason, John Mitchell. *Christian Mourning: A Sermon, Occasioned by the Death of Mrs. Isabella Graham.* New York: Whiting and Watson, 1814.

Power, John Carroll. *The Rise and Progress of Sunday Schools: A Biography of Robert Raikes and William Fox.* New York: Sheldon & Company, 1871.

Rice, Edwin Wilbur. *The Sunday-School Movement, 1817–1917.* Philadelphia: American Sunday-School Union, 1917.

Sarah Platt Doremus

Beaver, R. Pierce. *All Loves Excelling.* Grand Rapids: William B. Eerdmans Publishing Company, 1968.

Calkins, Gladys Gilkey. *Follow Those Women.* New York: National Council of Churches, United Church Women, 1961.

Daggett, Mrs. L. H. *Historical Sketches of Woman's Missionary Societies in America and England.* Boston: Published by the Author, [c. 1883].

Montgomery, Helen Barrett. *Western Women in Eastern Lands.* New York: The Macmillan Co., 1910.

Phoebe Palmer

Dayton, Donald W. *Discovering an Evangelical Heritage.* New York: Harper & Row, 1976.

Dayton, Donald W., and Dayton, Lucille Sider. "Women as Preachers: Evangelical Precedents." *Christianity Today,* 23 May 1975, pp. 4–7.

————. "'Your Daughters Shall Prophesy': Feminism in the Holiness Movement." *Methodist History* 14 (January 1976): 67–92.

Hughes, George. *The Beloved Physician, Walter C. Palmer, M.D.* New York: Palmer & Hughes, 1884.

————. *Fragrant Memories of the Tuesday Meeting and "The Guide to*

Holiness," and Their Fifty Years' Work for Jesus. New York: Palmer & Hughes, 1886.

Palmer, Phoebe. *Faith and Its Effects: or, Fragments from My Portfolio.* New York: Published for the Author, Joseph Longkin, Printer, 1852.

_____. *Promise of the Father; or, A Neglected Speciality of the Last Days.* Boston: Henry V. Degen, 1859.

_____. *The Way of Holiness.* New York: Foster and Palmer, Jr., 1867.

Palmer, Walter C., and Palmer, Phoebe. *Four Years in the Old World.* New York: Walter C. Palmer, Jr., Publisher, 1870.

Roche, John A. *The Life of Mrs. Sarah A. Lankford Palmer.* New York: George Hughes & Company, 1898.

Wheatley, Richard. *The Life and Letters of Mrs. Phoebe Palmer.* New York: W. C. Palmer, Jr., Publisher, 1876.

Elizabeth Prentiss

Prentiss, Elizabeth. *Religious Poems.* New York: Anson D. F. Randolph & Company, 1882.

_____. *Stepping Heavenward.* New York: N.P., 1869.

Prentiss, George L. *The Life and Letters of Elizabeth Prentiss.* New York: Anson D. F. Randolph & Company, 1882.

Antoinette Brown Blackwell

Blackwell, Antoinette Brown. *The Sexes Throughout Nature.* New York: G. P. Putnam's Sons, 1875.

Brown, Antoinette L. "Exegesis of 1 Corinthians, xiv., 34, 35; and I Timothy, ii., 11, 12." *Oberlin Quarterly Review* 3 (July 1849): 358–73.

Hays, Elinor Rice. *Those Extraordinary Blackwells.* New York: Harcourt, Brace & World, Inc., 1967.

Kerr, Laura. *Lady in the Pulpit.* New York: Woman's Press, 1951.

Lee, Luther. *Five Sermons and a Tract.* Edited by Donald W. Dayton. Chicago: Holrad House, 1975.

Catherine Mumford Booth

Begbie, Harold. *The Life of General William Booth.* 2 vols. New York: The Macmillan Company, 1920.

Booth, Catherine. *Aggressive Christianity.* Boston: The Christian Witness Co., 1899.

_____. *Female Ministry, or Woman's Right to Preach the Gospel.* London: Morgan & Chase, 1859; reprinted, New York: The Salvation Army Supplies Printing and Publishing Department, 1975.

Booth-Tucker, F. de L. *The Life of Catherine Booth: The Mother of the Salvation Army.* 2 vols. New York: Fleming H. Revell Company, 1892.

Frances Willard

Earhart, Mary. *Frances Willard: From Prayers to Politics.* Chicago: University of Chicago Press, 1944.

Strachey, Ray. *Frances Willard: Her Life and Work.* New York: Fleming H. Revell Company, 1913.

Trowbridge, Lydia Jones. *Frances Willard of Evanston.* Chicago: Willett, Clark & Company, 1938.

Willard, Frances E. *Glimpses of Fifty Years.* Chicago: Woman's Temperance Publication Association, H.J. Smith & Company, 1889.

––––––. *Woman and Temperance.* Hartford, Conn.: Park Publishing Co., 1883.

––––––. *Woman in the Pulpit.* Boston: D. Lothrop Company, 1888.

Amanda Smith

Smith, Amanda. *An Autobiography: The Story of the Lord's Dealings with Mrs. Amanda Smith.* Reprint edition, Noblesville, Ind.: Newby Book Room, 1972.

Ramabai

Butler, Clementina. *Pandita Ramabai Sarasvati.* New York: Fleming H. Revell Company, 1922.

Dyer, Helen S. *Pandita Ramabai: The Story of Her Life.* New York: Fleming H. Revell Company, 1900.

Foster, Warren Dunham, editor. *Heroines of Modern Religion.* New York: Sturgis & Walton Company, 1913.

Macnicol, Nicol. *Pandita Ramabai.* Calcutta: Association Press, 1926.

Ramabai. *The High-Caste Hindu Woman.* London: George Bell and Sons, 1888.

––––––. *Religious Consciousness of the Hindus.* Kedgaon, India: Mukti Mission Press, n.d.

––––––. *A Testimony.* Kedgaon, India: Mukti Mission Press, 1907.

Lucy Peabody and Helen Barrett Montgomery

Cattan, Louise Armstrong. *Lamps Are for Lighting.* Grand Rapids: William B. Eerdmans, 1972.

Montgomery, Helen Barrett. *Western Women in Eastern Lands.* New York: The Macmillan Co., 1910.